SOUP
for
TWO

Small-Batch Recipes for One, Two, or a Few

Joanna Pruess

SOUP

for

TWO

Small-Batch Recipes for One, Two, or a Few

Joanna Pruess

THE COUNTRYMAN PRESS · WOODSTOCK

Published by The Countryman Press, P.O. Box 748, Woodstock, VT 05091
Distributed by W. W. Norton & Company, Inc., 500 Fifth Avenue, New York, NY
10110
Printed in the United States

Soup for Two
ISBN 972-1-158157-228-5

10 9 8 7 6 5 4 3 2 1

All photography by Noah Fecks unless otherwise indicated.

Pg 6: PhotoSGH\Shutterstock; 22: Olha Afanasieva\Shutterstock;
25: Dora Zett\Shutterstock; 38: sarsmis\Shutterstock;
45: Lesya Dolyuk\Shutterstock; 50: Iryna Melnyk\Shutterstock;
55: Mariontxa\Shutterstock; 59: Maria Shumova\Shutterstock;
66: Anna Hoychuk\Shutterstock ;69, 131, 198: Brent Hofacker\Shutterstock;
85: Jiang Hongyan\Shutterstock; 86: Shaiith\Shutterstock;
91: B. and E. Dudzinscy\Shutterstock; 92: vanillachoes\Shutterstock;
99: zoryanchik\Shutterstock; 101: Alexandralaw1977\Shutterstock;
102: Dani Vincek\Shutterstock; 106, 126: Martin Turzak\Shutterstock;
110: Elena Elisseeva\Shutterstock; 113: Irina Zavyalova\Shutterstock;
115: Lensblur\istockphoto; 119: Nitr\Shutterstock;
120: Magdalena Paluchowska\Shutterstock;123: Yulia Davidovich\Shutterstock;
138: Natasha Breen\Shutterstock; 156: Marysckin\Shutterstock;
160: tiverlucky\Shutterstock; 167: Dzinnik Darius\Shutterstock;
201: voltan1\istockphoto; 204: Elena Shashkina\Shutterstock;

DEDICATION

I am grateful every single day for my extraordinary kids: Nicole, Ben, Justin, and Lindsey. They constantly amaze me and bring tremendous joy into my life. I look forward to sharing some of these soups with Jackson, my beautiful grandson, very soon.

INTRODUCTION | 10

BASICS | 15

CHILLED | 27

VEGETABLE | 63

LEGUME, NUT, AND BEAN | 105

SEAFOOD | 141

POULTRY | 163

MEAT | 193

ACKNOWLEDGMENTS | 218

INDEX | 220

SOUP

— *for* —

TWO

Small-Batch
Recipes
for One, Two,
or a Few

Joanna Pruess

INTRODUCTION

When England's Queen Victoria said, "Things taste better in small houses," she could have been speaking to twenty-first-century cooks who've downsized either by choice or by circumstances. Many of us have found we don't miss a lot of extra space, and, true to Victoria's words, our foods taste very, very good—maybe even better—in intimate surroundings. This is certainly true with soups, one of my favorite food categories. They are ideal to share with a partner or friend at the kitchen table, in an alcove, or in front of the TV.

Soup for Two was borne of my desire to create smaller amounts of delicious soups that for the most part are practical and easy to make. With no kids at home, limited refrigerator and freezer space, and zero desire to eat the same soup (no matter how tasty) several days running, I adapted favorite recipes and created several new ones that each make two 12-ounce mugs or bowls, or three 8-ounce cups.

You'll find traditional favorites like homey chicken-noodle soup, plus appealing variations from around the world, such as Lidia Bastianich's Nonna's Rice and Potato Soup, a treasured recipe from her grandmother in Friuli. "Legume, Nut, and Bean Soups" includes Nanny Annie's Barley-Mushroom Soup, in which Bette Shifman similarly pays homage to her Detroit-born grandmother. There's also a Vegetarian Split Pea Soup and a version with sausages.

No soup book would be complete without a tomato soup, and I include seven recipes that use different types and forms of tomatoes available today. Rainy Day Tomato Bisque relies on one of my newest go-to pantry staples: fire-roasted and petite-diced canned tomatoes. The soup was inspired by childhood days in my mom's kitchen. I serve it with grilled cheese triangles, a combo that still consoles me. Gazpacho, a staple in our house, uses plum tomatoes, and Chilled Summer Tomato

Soup with Pesto encourages you to seek just-picked produce from local farm stands.

Soups can be far more than familiar fare. Some recipes in Soup for Two were inspired by my travels: Finnish Jerusalem Artichoke Soup is a surprise in its simplicity yet rich, nutty flavor; Circassian Chicken Soup and Turkish Eggplant Soup are based on several visits to Turkey; and West African Peanut Soup with Chicken is easy to make and very satisfying.

Finally, most soups don't take a long time to make. When the vegetables or meat is tender, the soup is done. Many of the recipes in this book can be made in under an hour. To make them your own, you can add a final garnish (which can often be made ahead of time). Pumpernickel-Parmesan Croutons, Chile-Spiced Pumpkin Seeds, and Crunchy Chickpeas all dress up what's in these bowls and make them visually more exciting. One of the most important garnishes is that final sprinkle of fresh herbs. It's a small touch that makes a big difference.

I hope you enjoy making soup for two.

Joanna Pruess

BASICS

Equipment for a Small Kitchen | 16

At the Market | 19

In the Kitchen | 23

EQUIPMENT FOR A SMALL KITCHEN

Making about three cups of soup doesn't require a lot of cooking equipment. All of the soups in this book were made with the utensils below, most of which you probably already have.

- 2 ½-quart, 8-inch, heavy-bottomed saucepan
- 5-quart, 8-inch, heavy-bottomed pot
- Small and large strainers
- Silicon scrapers and wooden spoons
- Electric blender with 700 watts of power and a glass container of 56 ounces
- Food processor
- Flame tamer—useful to slowly sauté vegetables without burning them
- Good vegetable peeler
- Glass and metal measuring cups and spoons
- Oxo microplane—useful for thinly slicing onions and vegetables
- Sharp chef's knife and paring knife
- A couple of solid, fairly good-size LEXAN, acrylic, or bamboo cutting boards
- Deep fat or instant-read thermometer for frying
- Pepper mill
- Ladle, two soup bowls or mugs, and soup spoons

FOOD PROCESSORS VERSUS ELECTRIC BLENDERS: A PLACE FOR BOTH

Food processors operate at up to 1,700 rpms. They are ideal when you want a chunky-smooth texture and you have a high ratio of solids to liquids. If you ladle too much liquid (more than half full) into a processor's work bowl, it can rise to the top and ooze out. One way to avoid that is to use a slotted spoon when transferring cooked ingredients from the pot to the work bowl, leaving some of the broth in the pan. If needed, you can add more liquid to the bowl before the solids are returned to the pot.

Electric blenders spin at 17,000+, depending on the setting. They emulsify ingredients, holding them in suspension and creating that "velvety" finish. I don't think you need a lot of bells and whistles on the machine, but you do want one with about 400 watts that purées at lower and higher speeds. Although you can pulse ingredients in a blender, they often become too finely or unevenly chopped to sauté well. To avoid splattering soup on your ceiling or kitchen counters, start at a low speed when using a blender.

AT THE MARKET

Making soup for two means rethinking your shopping. Forget buying in bulk: You're wasting your money and storage space. Consider, instead, smaller-size jars, packages, and bottles. For example, many markets now sell stocks in both 16-ounce (2-cup) and 32-ounce (4-cup) boxes. Unless you'll use an opened box within about seven days, opt for less.

Large vegetables like butternut squash and fruits like watermelons are best bought cut up if you're not mindful about using them after you've made a soup. If they cost a little more, at least you won't throw out half of the product that's spoiled in the refrigerator. You also save prep time. Deli bars are often useful for a few sun-dried tomatoes, olives, and such. Family packs of highly perishable things like chicken make sense only if you separate them, put them in resealable plastic bags, and have the freezer space to store them.

THE CONVENIENCE OF SALAD BARS

Beyond the usual bite-size pieces of lettuce, tomato wedges, and onion rings, supermarket salad bars offer a huge array of vegetables, legumes, nuts, seasonal fruits, tofu, and cooked meats, as well as salad greens. At first glance, they may seem like a fine solution for small-portion soup cooking. Before you load up, however, take a minute to really look at these options.

First impressions count

What you see often indicates the quality of the salad bar, including how the food is handled behind the scenes.

- It should be well tended with appropriate utensils in place for each item.
- There should be no spillage.
- Food trays should be carefully set in, and a protective "sneeze" guard should extend upward or down from above to prevent shoppers from leaning over the food.
- Containers and lids, as well as dressings, should be neat and easily accessible.
- Empty trays should be refilled promptly. A high turnover is a good indication of freshness.

Cost and convenience

If you're buying only lettuce, radishes, and shredded carrots, $5.99 or $6.59 a pound seems extravagant. But add small amounts of olives, sun-dried tomatoes, or a handful of nuts that you'd otherwise have to buy in jars, then you're paying for the convenience of already prepared ingredients and enjoying the savings realized from buying smaller portions. For example, you don't have to buy a whole head of broccoli that may not be used in a timely fashion.

How to take your ingredients home

When buying several different ingredients from the salad bar, layer them in the container and try to carry them home carefully. Keep those that are marinated or in liquids in separate containers, unless they will ultimately be used in the same soup. With items that are prepacked, turn the container around completely before buying to make sure it's airtight.

TAKING STOCK

Stocks are arguably the most frequently used convenience foods. Unless you have lots of leftover bones and vegetables at your disposal, and plenty of time to simmer the pot, today's additive-free, lower-sodium stocks make great sense. The late, great chef Pierre Franey told me he always kept packaged stocks, along with canned beans and tomatoes, in his pantry.

Two to four cups of almost any purchased stock can be enriched with a small chopped carrot and celery rib, half a small onion, a few sprigs of fresh herbs, and a small bay leaf. If a soup's ingredients are already flavorful, however, such enrichment usually isn't needed. Stocks are basically conduits through which other flavors flow.

For vegetable stock, trimmings like the tops of leeks, papery skins from onions, and carrot peels enhance the flavor. The soaking liquid from dried mushrooms and the juice drained from canned tomatoes also can be used where appropriate for flavor.

It's important to note that almost all foods have a certain amount of sodium in them. When reducing stock, add salt only after tasting the finished soup. I generally start with ¼ teaspoon but add no more than ½ teaspoon. Let your own taste buds be your guide. My personal choice for cooking is fine or coarse sea salt rather than salts with chemicals like iodine and dextrose in them.

Because ingredients like noodles, grains, and beans are so porous, you should cook them before adding them, and then add them only at the end to warm them through.

It's always a good idea to keep some extra broth on hand to add if a soup is too thick.

IN THE KITCHEN

MEASURING

In these recipes, I've use volumetric measurements rather than just a number for the ingredients, because it's hard to quantify exactly what a medium-size carrot or onion is. In large pots of soup, amounts are flexible, and it generally doesn't matter if you make a little more or less. When starting out, I want you to feel comfortable making recipes that yield about three cups. As a guide, figure one medium carrot or celery rib roughly equals ½ to ⅓ a cup diced or chopped. A smaller one is ¼ to ⅓ cup. A small onion equals ½ to ⅔ cup; a large onion is ¾ to one cup.

Once you're used to my recipes, you can eyeball the quantities and, even more important, tweak them to your taste. If you make soup often, you can finely chop or dice a few carrots, ribs of celery, and onions and refrigerate them in covered containers for at least three days. Then you can measure out ½ or ⅓ cup of each vegetable as specified in the recipe.

CUTTING AND CHOPPING VEGETABLES

Almost every soup requires cutting and chopping ingredients. While you don't need several knives—I mostly use a six- or eight-inch chef's knife and a paring knife—they should be sharpened regularly to be effective. At home, you can use a sharpening steel, a stone, or a home sharpener. I also try to take mine to a professional grinder at least once every few months. I can't emphasze how important it is to take care of your knives. You'll be amazed how much easier and safer it is to slice and dice with a sharp knife that doesn't slip. Below are tips on cutting up some common ingredients:

CARROTS: Once they are scraped and the ends trimmed, cut each carrot into two or three pieces of the same length. Using a large chef's knife, cut the pieces in half lengthwise, so they lie flat on a cutting board, and cut them into thin or thicker batons, according to what the recipe calls for; then turn and chop the pieces crosswise into whatever size you want.

CELERY: After a rib is trimmed at the top and bottom (the leaves may be reserved to add flavor to stock), it can be sliced or diced. Either slice it crosswise or run the tip of a knife down the length of the rib, and cut crosswise into cubes.

ONIONS: The easiest way I know to slice or chop onions is to cut off a narrow slice at the top and bottom, made a small incision along the side, through the skin and one layer of the onion, and remove. Then cut off a thin slice from one side, creating a flat base so that the onion will not slip or rock as it is being cut.

To slice: Place the flat, cut part on the cutting board and make even slices almost through the onion, working from the right (or left) to the center. Once at the center, turn the onion 180 degrees and slice the other half, holding the first slices together against the middle so that all the slices are equally thick or thin.

To chop: Trim off the top and the smallest amount from the root end. The onion should stand steady. You don't need to slice off anything from the side (as above). Cutting from the top down, make narrow or wide slices almost to the root. Turn the onion 45 degrees and slice the onion, again almost to the root. In the center, cut the onion through the root end and, with the flat center on the cutting board, slice the onion into pieces, working from the top to the root end.

PARSNIPS: While similar in shape to carrots, and cut up in the same manner, parsnips tend to be tougher, and a sharp knife is essential.

BELL PEPPERS: There are several ways to remove the membranes and seeds before slicing or dicing bell peppers. This is my favorite. Most peppers have three to five indented ridges running from top to bottom that correspond to the membranes inside. Starting at either end, slice off large pieces of the pepper just to the left and right along either side of the ridges. You will end up with tapered rectangular pieces and a birdcage of membranes and the seeds to discard. Using a sharp knife, I prefer to slice or dice the pieces with the skin side up.

USE EVERY PART OF THE VEGETABLE

Anyone mindful of food costs knows that soups can provide inexpensive, nourishing meals, and humble ingredients often add up to far more than the sum of their modest parts. For example, the Leftover Root Vegetable Soup combines stock with bits and bobs of carrots, turnips, parsnips, and any other roots that may be withering in your refrigerator. Add ras al hanout, a Moroccan spice mixture, along with some oil-cured olives, and the mixture is elevated to an exotic dish.

Even the tops of radishes or beets can be used for soup. Simmer radish greens with potato into a simple soup that tastes like sorrel. It can be served with a dollop of Greek yogurt. I make it a bit more stylish with toasted hazelnuts and a drizzle of hazelnut oil.

Many simple soups turn into more substantial offerings with the addition of leftover meat, poultry, fish, or tofu. Cooked turkey from Thanksgiving or any another time enriches barley and spinach soup; and leftover grilled salmon (or a piece purchased at the take-out counter) could become Salmon and Corn Chowder in minutes with the aid of frozen or cooked corn.

Speaking of leftovers, throughout *Soup for Two* I've indicated where you can use some of the extra ingredients from one soup to the next. If you make Provençal Tomato-Fennel Soup with Saffron, the remaining fennel can be used in the exciting dessert Morello Cherry Soup with Candied Ginger and Fennel.

Quick Vegetable Soup

To make a quick vegetable soup for two, choose an assortment of basic vegetables, such as tomatoes, zucchini slices, shredded carrots, sliced celery, onion slices, chickpeas, and kidney beans. At home, place them in a medium-size saucepan with beef or chicken broth to cover, season with salt and pepper to taste and with whatever dried herbs you have on hand (perhaps thyme and basil). Simmer, partially covered, for an hour or so. Ten minutes before serving, you might want to stir in two to three tablespoons of orzo or other small pasta. Add more stock as needed, finish cooking, taste for seasonings, and serve with crisp bread.

CHILLED

Chilled Strawberry-Ginger Soup | 28

Blueberry-Pomegranate Beet Borscht | 31

Peach Soup with Sugar-Glazed Blackberries | 32

Pineapple Soup with Blueberries and Toasted Coconut | 35

Morello Cherry Soup with Candied Ginger and Fennel | 36

Watermelon Gazpacho Soup | 39

Chilled Fire-Roasted Tomato Bisque | 40

Chilled Summer Tomato Soup with Pesto | 43

Puréed Avocado Soup with Guacamole Toppings | 47

Roasted Beet Soup with Dukkah, Yogurt, and Black Currant | 48

Curried Cucumber and Scallion Soup | 51

Cauliflower-Cashew Soup with Pomegranate Seeds | 53

Andalusian Garlic-Almond Soup | 54

Minted Spiced Green Pea Soup with Crunchy Chickpeas | 57

Gazpacho | 60

Cucumber-Watercress Soup with Diced Tomatoes | 61

CHILLED STRAWBERRY-GINGER SOUP

This beautiful and healthy fruit soup is quick and easy to make and full of flavor. Along with ripe berries, it's sweetened with minced, candied ginger, vanilla yogurt, and fresh orange juice. Serve a cup and a half of the soup for a light, warm-weather entrée or a cup as an appetizer or dessert. You can substitute other juices or even coconut milk for part of the liquid.

1 pound strawberries, hulled, 1 small berry reserved for garnish

1 cup low-fat vanilla yogurt, plus ¼ cup for garnish

¼ cup orange juice, preferably freshly squeezed

2 tablespoons minced candied ginger (about 1 ounce)

3 tablespoons chopped mint leaves, plus 4 small leaves for garnish

In the jar of an electric blender, combine the strawberries, 1 cup yogurt, orange juice, and ginger and purée until completely smooth. Chill for at least 1 hour.

Meanwhile, in a small bowl, combine the remaining yogurt with the chopped mint leaves and, using a muddler or the back of a spoon, crush the leaves to release their flavor; set aside.

Ladle the soup into chilled bowls. Strain the minted yogurt into a small cup. Spoon a generous dollop of the strained yogurt in the center of each bowl of soup. Slice the reserved berry lengthwise. Place a few slices on the yogurt, add two small mint leaves, and serve.

BLUEBERRY-POMEGRANATE BEET BORSCHT

Blueberries and pomegranates are excellent antioxidants. Add to them the anti-aging, cancer-preventing, cardiovascular-invigorating benefits of beets (not to mention their reputation as an aphrodisiac), and this innovative cold borscht might well become a new favorite. It was inspired by a conversation with cookbook author and friend Linda Dannenberg. The flavor is very intense. Serve it as an appetizer or chilled summer soup. Garnished with scallions, a dollop of sour cream, and fresh pomegranate seeds. It's beautiful, as well.

2¾ cups natural blueberry-pomegranate juice

1–2 tablespoons pomegranate molasses, available at Middle Eastern stores and many markets

½ cup cubed pickled beets

1–2 tablespoons sour cream

1 tablespoon fresh pomegranate seeds, for garnish

1 tablespoon thinly sliced scallion, for garnish

In a large bowl, stir the blueberry-pomegranate juice and 1 tablespoon of the pomegranate molasses together until blended. Stir in the beets, taste, and add more pomegranate molasses, if desired. Chill well. Ladle into two bowls and serve with a dollop of sour cream, the pomegranate seeds, and sliced scallions.

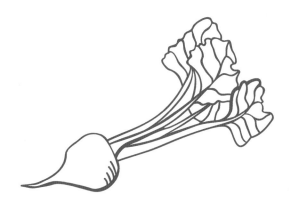

PEACH SOUP WITH SUGAR-GLAZED BLACKBERRIES

When the dog days of summer have you avoiding the kitchen, yet looking for a refreshing dessert of seasonal fruit, this subtle, spicy chilled soup will please you and your guests. It's dressed up with sugar-glazed fresh blackberries (made the night before) that add a crunchy, special accent. Don't use nonfat yogurt, because the soup will taste too thin.

½ cup granulated sugar

8-10 fresh, unblemished blackberries

1 egg white

2 peaches, peeled and finely chopped or 1 pound unsweetened frozen peaches, defrosted (2 cups)

1 cup natural apple cider

2 tablespoons honey

1 tablespoon freshly squeezed lime juice

¼ teaspoon ground star anise

¼ teaspoon ground cinnamon

6 ounces low-fat vanilla yogurt

Mint leaves for garnish

Make the sugar-glazed blackberries at least 8 hours ahead of time. Line a baking sheet with parchment. Pour the sugar into a flat dish. Using a small paintbrush, lightly coat each berry with egg white, carefully roll it in the sugar, and place on the parchment. Let them dry for at least 6 hours in a cool, dry place. Once dried, the coated berries keep for many hours.

For the soup: In the jar of an electric blender, combine the peaches, cider, honey, lime juice, star anise, and cinnamon and purée until smooth. Pour into a bowl, blend in the yogurt, cover, and chill for at least 2 hours. Ladle the soup into bowls, add the blackberries, and garnish with a few mint leaves.

PINEAPPLE SOUP WITH BLUEBERRIES AND TOASTED COCONUT

With a fresh pineapple on my counter and an opened can of coconut milk and fresh ginger root in the refrigerator, necessity sparked my creative instincts. This easy-to-make dessert was the delicious result. You can buy cut-up pineapple or, in a pinch, use canned fruit packed in its own juice. Coconut ice cream, fresh blueberries, and toasted coconut flakes added before serving make this soup a special treat. It tastes like a piña colada.

3 cups cut-up fresh pineapple (about 12 ounces)

¾ cup canned coconut milk, not "lite" variety

1 tablespoon grated fresh ginger root

2–3 tablespoons light brown sugar

1 tablespoon Jamaican rum

½ cup fresh blueberries

Coconut ice cream

2 tablespoons toasted coconut flakes for garnish

In the jar of an electric blender, combine the pineapple, coconut milk, ginger, 2 tablespoons of the brown sugar, and the rum; purée until completely smooth. Taste and add more sugar if desired. Ladle into bowls, add the blueberries and a small scoop of ice cream. Sprinkle on the coconut and serve.

To Cut a Pineapple:

Using a serrated knife, cut off the leafy crown of the pineapple and about an inch from the bottom. Place the pineapple on a solid cutting board and slice off the skin in strips. With the tip of a potato peeler or paring knife, remove the brown eyes. Cut the pineapple in quarters lengthwise and cut off the woody center core.

MORELLO CHERRY SOUP WITH CANDIED GINGER AND FENNEL

Combining preserved cherries and fennel sounds unusual, but I think you'll find this a delicious dessert. Years ago, I wrote about Thaddeus DuBois, who was, for a while, a White House chef. The memory of his candied fennel ice cream stuck with me. When I was given a 21-ounce jar of Fabbri Morello cherries in kirsch syrup, I decided to marry the flavors. Fennel is very popular in Italy, where Morello cherries are grown. The cherries are available here in gourmet stores or via the Internet.

2 tablespoons unsalted butter

1¼ cups finely chopped fennel (about ½ medium fennel bulb), some fronds reserved for garnish

½ cup finely chopped shallots

2 tablespoons minced candied ginger

2 teaspoons ground star anise or fennel

Generous pinch kosher salt

1¼ cups drained, pitted Morello cherries in kirsch syrup, plus 10 cherries reserved for garnish

1½ cups buttermilk

½ cup heavy cream

In a medium saucepan, melt the butter. Stir in the fennel, shallots, ginger, star anise or fennel seeds, and salt. Cover and sweat over low heat until the fresh fennel is very soft, 10–12 minutes, stirring occasionally,

Add the cherries and buttermilk and heat gently, stirring up all cooked bits. Do not let it boil. Scrape the mixture into the jar of an electric blender and purée until completely smooth. Pour the soup into a bowl, stir in the heavy cream, 1–2 teaspoons of the reserved cherry syrup, or to taste, and refrigerate until cold. Ladle the soup into bowls, add the reserved cherries and a few fennel fronds, and serve.

WATERMELON GAZPACHO SOUP

Chef Joy Strang's gazpacho is an exciting, refreshing summer soup. With the convenience of peeled and diced watermelon available in many markets, this beautiful chilled soup takes minutes to make. The rewards are great. You can garnish it simply with crumbled feta cheese, or for a singular treat add fresh crabmeat.

3 cups diced seedless or seeded watermelon

10 mint leaves, coarsely chopped

1 medium clove garlic

½ jalapeño pepper, seeded if desired, and chopped

1 tablespoon freshly squeezed lime juice

1 tablespoon sherry vinegar

1 teaspoon smoked paprika, plus a little more for garnish

½ teaspoon ground allspice

Salt

4 ounces jumbo lump crabmeat (optional)

2 scallions, white and pale green parts, thinly sliced for garnish

Crumbled feta for garnish

In the jar of an electric blender, combine the watermelon, mint leaves, garlic, jalapeño, lime juice, vinegar, paprika, and allspice. Blend on medium until completely smooth. Season to taste with salt and pulse briefly. Scrape the gazpacho into a bowl, cover, and chill for at least 3 hours before serving.

If adding crab, divide it between two bowls and pour in the gazpacho. Garnish with scallions, feta, and a light sprinkle of paprika and serve.

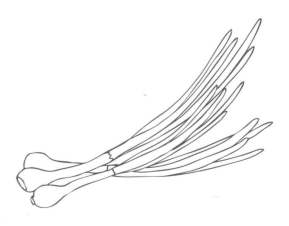

CHILLED FIRE-ROASTED
TOMATO BISQUE

Thanks to readily available, intensely flavorful fire-roasted canned tomatoes, Pam Harding's refreshing cold soup is an easy answer to the question of what to serve on a hot summer's evening. Keep a supply of these tomatoes in your cupboard for many different soups. Canned chipotles en adobo are smoked jalapeños packed in adobo sauce (see the sidebar). Because chipotles are spicy, add only half the amount at first.

1 tablespoon canola or other
    vegetable oil

1 small carrot, finely chopped
    (¼ cup)

½ medium celery rib, chopped
    (¼ cup)

1 very small onion or half medium
    onion, finely chopped (¼ cup)

1 large clove garlic, minced

1½ cups chicken stock

1 cup canned fire-roasted petite
    diced tomatoes

1 tablespoon tomato paste

1 small chipotle chile en adobo,
    minced (1 teaspoon)

½ teaspoon ground cumin

½ teaspoon dried oregano, crushed

½–1 teaspoon sugar (optional)

⅓ cup 2 percent buttermilk

2 tablespoons torn cilantro leaves

In a medium-size saucepan, heat the oil over medium heat. Add the carrot, celery, and onion and sauté until wilted, 4–5 minutes, stirring occasionally. Stir in the garlic and cook for 30 seconds.

Add the stock, tomatoes, tomato paste, chipotle, cumin, and oregano and bring to a boil. Reduce the heat, cover, and simmer until the vegetables are tender, 15–20 minutes. If the soup tastes too sharp, stir in ½–1 teaspoon sugar, and refrigerate for at least an hour. Before serving, stir in the buttermilk and sprinkle on the cilantro.

Adobo Sauce

In Mexican cooking, this tangy combination of chiles, garlic, and vinegar along with tomatoes and spices is widely used as a marinade or sauce to season meat or poultry dishes. It first arrived in the New World with the Spaniards.

CHILLED SUMMER TOMATO SOUP
WITH PESTO

This smooth red purée celebrates the peak of the summer tomato-growing season. The cool but not cold soup is topped with basil pesto or pistou (page 44). Here is the place to use very juicy heirloom or seasonal beefsteak tomatoes found at local farmers' markets.

1 tablespoon fragrant extra-virgin olive oil

1 medium-small onion, thinly sliced (½ cup)

1 small carrot, diced (¼ cup)

½ medium celery rib, diced (¼ cup)

White part of 1 medium leek, well rinsed, cut in half lengthwise and thinly sliced (¼ cup)

½ small red bell pepper, diced (¼ cup)

2 large cloves garlic, sliced

4–5 large fresh basil leaves

1 sprig flat-leaf parsley

1 small sprig rosemary

1 small sprig thyme

1 teaspoon fennel seeds

1 pound firm, ripe heirloom or beefsteak tomatoes, cored and roughly chopped

1½ cups water

Salt and white pepper

2 tablespoons Brice's Homemade Basil Pesto (recipe follows) or a high quality purchased product

In a medium-size saucepan, heat the oil over medium heat. Stir in the onion, carrot, celery, leek, bell pepper, and garlic cloves. Cover and sweat over low heat until the vegetables are tender but not brown, about 7 minutes, stirring occasionally.

Meanwhile, wrap the basil, parsley, rosemary, thyme, and fennel seeds in two layers of cheesecloth; tie securely. Add the tomatoes, water, and herbs to the pan, cover, and gently boil until the tomatoes are soft, 12-15 minutes. Remove the herbs, squeezing any liquid into the pan.

Fill a large bowl with ice. Transfer the tomato-vegetable mixture to a bowl and set it over the ice to cool, about 20 minutes, to keep the color bright. Scrape the mixture into the jar of an electric blender and purée until completely smooth. Pour through a strainer, pressing firmly with a silicon spatula to extract as much liquid as possible. Season with salt and pepper to taste, cover, and refrigerate until cool. Ladle into bowls, add basil pesto, and serve.

Bruce's Homemade Basil Pesto

Yield: about 1 cup

My friend Bruce Robertson seems to have a never-ending source of wonderfully fragrant basil pesto. Of course, he also has a variety of local farm stands near his house on the North Fork of Long Island. He suggests using whichever variety of basil you have: Italian, bush, or lemon—or a mix. He also says you can add a couple of tablespoons of flat-leaf parsley leaves. Extra basil will last in your refrigerator for several weeks. You can make a smoother pesto by combining the ingredients in an electric blender, scraping down the sides often, before adding the oil.

2 cloves garlic

2 cups basil leaves (see the headnote)

⅓ cup grated Parmigiano-Reggiano

⅓ cup grated Pecorino-Romano

¼ cup pine nuts

⅛ teaspoon freshly grated black pepper

2 tablespoons fragrant extra-virgin olive oil

In a food processor, pulse the garlic until finely chopped. Add a handful of the basil along with the cheeses, pine nuts, and pepper; pulse until finely chopped. Add the remaining basil, a little at a time, pulsing after each addition until finely chopped. Finally, with the motor running, add the oil and blend into a smooth consistency. Scrape into a container, cover tightly, and refrigerate if not using right away.

PURÉED AVOCADO SOUP WITH GUACAMOLE TOPPINGS

If you love guacamole, try adding stock and a little sour cream to transform the same ingredients into a lovely, cooling summer soup. To turn it into a main course, add grilled chicken or shrimp on top. For a smokier flavor, use mezcal rather than tequila.

1 small onion

1 ripe avocado, preferably Hass variety, peeled and pitted (about ½ pound)

1 small clove garlic

2 tablespoons freshly squeezed lime juice

1½ teaspoons hot or mild chile powder

1 teaspoon ground cumin

½ teaspoon salt or to taste

Freshly ground black pepper

¾–1 cup vegetable stock

2 tablespoons sour cream, plus additional sour cream for garnish

1 tablespoon tequila or mezcal (optional)

½ plum tomato, seeded and finely chopped (3 tablespoons)

1 jalapeño pepper, minced, seeded if desired (2 tablespoons)

3 tablespoons chopped cilantro leaves, plus a few leaves for garnish

Tortilla chips for garnish (optional)

Dice about ¾ of the onion. In a food processor or the jar of an electric blender, combine the avocado, the diced onion, garlic, lime juice, chile powder, cumin, salt, black pepper to taste, and about ¾ cup of stock; purée until smooth. Add the sour cream and tequila or mezcal and blend, adding the remaining stock if the soup is too thick. Scrape into a bowl and chill.

Before serving, finely chop the remaining ¼ onion by hand. Blend it with the tomato, jalapeño, and cilantro leaves and stir into the soup. Taste to adjust the seasonings. Ladle the soup into bowls, garnish with a dollop of sour cream, a few cilantro leaves, and serve with tortilla chips, if desired.

The Avocado Fruit

Many people think avocados are vegetables, but with a large pit inside, they're actually fruits. I grew up in Los Angeles with an avocado tree in our backyard and still think the locally grown Hass avocados are the best. Many chefs agree. They have a creamier, denser texture than other varieties.

ROASTED BEET SOUP WITH DUKKAH, YOGURT, AND BLACK CURRANT

While in Bath, England, my daughter Nicole, son Ben, and I celebrated my birthday at a renowned vegetarian restaurant founded by chef Rachel DeMuth. It's now owned by her chef and renamed Acorn. Ben's earthy, roasted beet salad with cassis sorbet was seasoned with dukkah, an Egyptian seasoning made of toasted nuts, sesame seeds, coriander, and cumin. It inspired this soup. Instead of the sorbet, I boiled currant jelly with balsamic vinegar to make a gastrique-like drizzle (typically made with reduced vinegar and caramelized sugar).

1 tablespoon dukkah (recipe follows)

3 medium beets, scrubbed and trimmed

2 tablespoons fragrant extra-virgin olive oil

Salt and freshly ground pepper

1 small onion, chopped (⅓ cup)

2–2½ cups vegetable stock

2 tablespoons orange juice

1 small shallot, sliced

3 tablespoons balsamic vinegar

3 tablespoons black or red currant jelly

2 tablespoons water

2–3 tablespoons plain Greek yogurt

Preheat the oven to 400 degrees F.

Prepare the dukkah and set aside.

On a large square of aluminum foil, brush the beets with a little olive oil, season with salt and pepper, and tightly wrap to seal. Place on a baking sheet or in a flat pan and roast until completely tender when pricked with the tip of a knife, at least 50–60 minutes. Remove, cool, peel, and roughly chop. You should have just under 2 cups.

In a small skillet, heat 1 tablespoon of the oil over low heat, add the onion, partially cover, and sweat until softened and just starting to color, about 5 minutes. Scrape into the jar of an electric blender along with the puréed beets, stock, and ½ tablespoon of the olive oil; purée until smooth. Transfer to a medium-size saucepan, add the orange juice; heat until hot.

Meanwhile, make the gastrique. In the same skillet, add the remaining oil and shallot and sauté over low heat until softened and lightly colored. Combine the shallot with the 3 tablespoons of balsamic vinegar, the currant jelly, and water in a 2-cup glass measure and microwave on high until the mixture has reduced by half, about 4 minutes. Remove and strain.

To serve, ladle the soup into bowls, add a dollop of yogurt, sprinkle the dukkah around it, and drizzle on the currant gastrique.

Dukkah

Dukkah can be made with pistachios, hazelnuts, and even almonds. Use the freshest spices available and store extras in a small, airtight container. If your nuts are unsalted, add a pinch of salt to the mixture.

1 tablespoon sesame seeds

¼ teaspoon coarsely ground black pepper or crushed black peppercorns

¼ teaspoon fennel seeds

1 teaspoon ground coriander

1 teaspoon ground cumin

¼ cup chopped pistachios, lightly toasted (1½ ounces)

Salt, if nuts are unsalted

In a small skillet, toast the sesame seeds, black pepper, and fennel over medium-high heat until fragrant and the seeds are pale golden, 2–3 minutes, shaking the pan often. Sprinkle in the coriander and cumin, cook for 30 seconds, then quickly scrape into a small bowl along with the pistachios and salt and let cool. Using a mortar and pestle or a clean coffee grinder, grind the mixture into a coarse-textured powder.

Delights of Dukkah

My friends Sarah and Glenn Collins are world travelers, and we delight in sharing our culinary purchases with one another. After exploring Egypt's Nile Valley some years ago, Sarah gave me a bag of dukkah, a term derived from a word that means "to crush." In this case, it refers to seeds and nuts. I've used it as a topping for many soups, combined with olive oil as a dip for bread, and brushed it on fish and chicken. Thanks, Sarah!

CURRIED CUCUMBER AND SCALLION SOUP

Thai red curry paste combined with cucumber and scallions makes for a mildly spicy yet cooling partnership in this soup. It's refreshing and easy. You can also use Malaysian or Indian curry paste, adjusting the amount according to taste.

1 English cucumber, ends trimmed

8 scallions, chopped, including most of the green parts (1½ cups)

¾ cup vegetable broth

½ cup sour cream, plus 2 teaspoons for garnish

2–3 teaspoons freshly squeezed lemon juice

½ teaspoon grated lemon zest

½ teaspoon Thai red curry paste (see headnote on page 157)

Salt

1 tablespoon chopped fresh dill leaves, plus 2 small sprigs for garnish

Cut off two thin slices of cucumber and reserve for the garnish. Peel and roughly chop the remaining cucumber and add it to the jar of an electric blender along with the scallions, broth, sour cream, 2 teaspoons lemon juice, lemon zest, curry paste, and salt to taste. Process until smooth.

Stir in the dill, cover, and refrigerate until chilled, about 1 hour. Taste and add more lemon juice, if needed. Ladle the soup into two bowls. Add a small spoonful of sour cream, a slice of cucumber, and a sprig of dill to each and serve.

CAULIFLOWER-CASHEW SOUP WITH POMEGRANATE SEEDS

Cauliflower roasted with chopped onion, garlic, and curry powder and then puréed with softened raw cashews and coconut milk creates a creamy, rich soup without any dairy products. Many markets now sell peeled pomegranate seeds, making them an attractive and easy garnish for this pale golden soup. Use extras in the Blueberry-Pomegranate Beet Borscht (page 31), salads, and on sautéed vegetables. You can serve this soup chilled, at room temperature, or hot.

⅓ cup raw cashews

2 cups (about 7 ounces) small cauliflower florets

1 small onion, chopped (⅓ cup)

1 large clove garlic, chopped

Salt

1 tablespoon vegetable oil

2 teaspoons ground curry powder, hot or mild, according to taste

½ teaspoon ground cumin

1½ cups vegetable stock

¾ cup canned coconut milk, not "lite" variety

1½ teaspoons honey

Pinch ground cayenne pepper (optional)

2 tablespoons pomegranate seeds (optional)

1 tablespoon torn cilantro leaves

Preheat the oven to 400 degrees F. Line a baking sheet with aluminum foil.

In a small bowl, pour enough boiling water over the cashews to cover; set aside to soften, at least 45 minutes.

Meanwhile, in a bowl, stir together the cauliflower, onion, garlic, about ½ teaspoon salt, and the oil, turning to coat evenly. Scrape onto the baking sheet and roast in the center of the oven until the cauliflower is completely tender when the tip of a knife is inserted, 20–25 minutes, stirring once or twice. Carefully sprinkle on the curry powder and cumin, stir, and roast for 2 minutes longer.

Strain the cashews, rinse under cold water, and transfer them to the jar of an electric blender. Add the stock and purée on high until completely smooth.

Scrape the cauliflower mixture into the blender, add the coconut milk, honey, and cayenne if using, and purée until completely smooth, scraping down the sides as needed. Taste to adjust the salt, if needed.

Scrape into a clean container, cover, and refrigerate for 30 minutes–1 hour. Ladle into bowls, sprinkle on the pomegranate seeds if using, add the cilantro, and serve.

ANDALUSIAN GARLIC-ALMOND SOUP

Ajo blanco, this classic cold white Spanish soup of puréed garlic, bread, and almonds with a dash of sherry vinegar, is a perfect antidote to sweltering summer days. My kids and I were introduced to it during a cooking class in Seville with Amelia Gómez.

Grapes are the traditional garnish to balance the garlic, but small cubes of watermelon or apple are also used today. The soup is said to have originated in the Roman colony of Hispalis (today's Seville), where almond milk was consumed in large amounts. For another cold gazpacho, look at the one on page 39 made with watermelon.

2 cups stale or lightly toasted country bread, crusts removed, torn in pieces

1⅓ cups cold water, plus ½ cup additional water if needed

¾ cup blanched almonds

1½–2 cloves garlic

⅓ cup fruity extra-virgin olive oil, preferably Spanish

1½ teaspoons Spanish sherry vinegar, or to taste

Salt

About 10 red or green seedless grapes, cut in half, or small cubes of watermelon for garnish.

In a bowl, combine the bread with 1⅓ cups water and soak until softened, about 5 minutes. Remove the bread and squeeze gently, reserving the water. Combine the bread with the almonds and garlic in a food processor and pulse until chunky-smooth. Add the water and blend until smooth.

With the motor running, pour in the olive oil and blend. Add the vinegar and ½ teaspoon salt or to taste; process until the mixture is thin and smooth. Taste to adjust the flavors, adding up to ½ cup more water, as needed. Transfer to a bowl, cover, and refrigerate until cold. Ladle the soup into two bowls, add the grapes or watermelon, and serve.

Early Spanish Soup History

Ajo Blanco dates from long before gazpacho. It's from the period when the Romans ruled the Iberian Peninsula before the Christian era and far before Columbus brought tomatoes back to Spain in the 16th century.

MINTED SPICED GREEN PEA SOUP WITH CRUNCHY CHICKPEAS

This refreshing light soup with its subtle taste of curry (more potent if you use hot curry powder and/or the cayenne) is nicely balanced by the final addition of mint leaves and crunchy chickpeas. Fair warning: The chickpeas are irresistible. Make the whole recipe, and any leftovers will be gone pronto.

1 tablespoon canola or other vegetable oil

1 medium onion, chopped (½ cup)

1 large clove garlic, finely chopped

1½ teaspoons mild or hot curry powder, according to taste

½ teaspoon ground cardamom

1½ cups chicken or vegetable stock

1 cup frozen peas, defrosted

1 medium-small Yukon Gold or other waxy potato, diced (¾ cup)

¾ cup whole milk

Salt and finely ground black pepper

Pinch cayenne pepper (optional)

Crunchy Chickpeas (recipe follows)

1 tablespoon julienned mint leaves

In a medium-size saucepan, heat the oil over medium heat. Add the onion and sauté until tender and lightly colored, about 4 minutes, stirring occasionally. Add the garlic and cook for 30 seconds. Stir in the curry powder and cardamom, cook for 1 minute, then stir in the stock.

Add the peas and potatoes and bring the liquid to a boil. Reduce the heat, cover, and gently boil until the vegetables are tender, 10–15 minutes. Transfer the ingredients to the jar of an electric blender, add the milk, and purée until completely smooth. Season to taste with salt, pepper, and cayenne if using. Refrigerate for at least 30 minutes or until cool.

Meanwhile, prepare the Crunchy Chickpeas, if serving. Ladle the soup into bowls, add the chickpeas, sprinkle on the mint leaves, and serve.

Crunchy Chickpeas

You can add a few of these to each bowl of soup. But don't worry about having made too many—these make a wonderful snack anytime. Keep them stored in an airtight container.

1 teaspoon fennel seeds

1 large shallot, very thinly sliced

2 tablespoons all-purpose flour

1½–2 cups canola or other vegetable oil for frying

1 cup canned chickpeas, rinsed and patted dry

½ teaspoon Aleppo pepper

Kosher salt

Freshly ground black pepper

In a small, dry skillet, toast the fennel seeds until golden brown, about 2 minutes, shaking the pan occasionally. Set aside.

Lightly toss the shallots with flour to cover. In a medium-size pot, heat the oil until it measures 350 degrees F, on an instant-read thermometer. Add the shallots and cook over medium-high heat until golden brown, 3–4 minutes. Remove with a slotted spoon to paper towels to drain.

Return the oil to 350 degrees F. Add the chickpeas and cook until crispy and golden brown. Depending on how wide the pot is, it can take 5–12 minutes. Remove with a slotted spoon to a metal or glass bowl. Add the Aleppo pepper and salt and freshly ground pepper to taste. Toss well and serve.

GAZPACHO

Although chilled gazpacho is now a summer staple, food historians tell us tomatoes arrived in Spain only after Columbus brought the seeds back from the New World. They definitely weren't an instant success and were even considered poisonous.

It's worth peeling and finely dicing the tomatoes by hand for this soup, because the colors remain more vibrant and the texture is better. Unless you eat a lot of cucumbers, a small pickling cucumber is all you'll need here. Another refreshing gazpacho, made with watermelon, is on page 39.

3 plum tomatoes (about 12 ounces), cored, with a small "X" cut in the bottom

¾–1 cup tomato juice

½ cup peeled, seeded, and finely diced cucumber (see the headnote)

1 small red onion, finely diced (⅓ cup)

1 small yellow, orange, or red bell pepper, finely diced (⅓ cup)

1 clove garlic, minced

½ small jalapeño pepper, seeded and minced

2 tablespoons fragrant extra-virgin olive oil

1 tablespoon freshly squeezed lime juice

2 teaspoons Worcestershire sauce

Salt and freshly ground black pepper

¼ cup coarsely chopped cilantro leaves

Fill a bowl with ice water. Bring a small pot of water to a boil, drop in the tomatoes, and boil for 20 seconds. Using a slotted spoon, transfer the tomatoes to the ice water, cool for about 1 minute, then peel, cut in half crosswise, and using a spoon, scoop out the seeds.

Cut the tomato into small cubes and put into a bowl. Stir in ¾ cup of the tomato juice. Add the cucumber, onion, bell pepper, garlic, jalapeño, olive oil, lime juice, and Worcestershire sauce. Season to taste with salt and pepper and add the remaining tomato juice, if needed. Cover and refrigerate for at least 1–2 hours to let the flavors develop. Ladle into chilled bowls, add the cilantro, and serve.

CUCUMBER-WATERCRESS SOUP WITH DICED TOMATOES

Here's another appealing summer offering. This intensely vibrant, green chilled soup flecked with diced tomato takes minimal work. It was inspired by a recipe from famed cookbook author Carole Walter. The small amount of sour cream at the end definitely rounds out all of the flavors.

1½ cucumbers, peeled, seeded, and diced (3 cups)

2 cups packed watercress sprigs with coarse stems trimmed

¾ cup plain low-fat yogurt

1 tablespoon extra-virgin olive oil, plus a little to drizzle before serving

1½ tablespoons sour cream (optional)

1 tablespoon freshly squeezed lime juice

1½ plum tomatoes, finely chopped (½ cup)

2 tablespoons chopped fresh basil

2 tablespoons snipped fresh chives

Salt and freshly ground black pepper

In the jar of an electric blender, combine the cucumbers, watercress, and yogurt, and purée until smooth. Do this in batches if necessary.

Pour the soup into a bowl, stir in the olive oil, sour cream, if using, and lime juice. Stir in the tomatoes, basil, chives, and season with salt and pepper to taste. Cover and chill for at least 1 hour. Ladle into bowls, drizzle on a little olive oil, and serve.

VEGETABLE

Butternut Squash Soup with Mole and Peppers | 64

Carrot-Ginger Soup with Chèvre | 67

Green Bean–Mushroom Soup with Frizzled Onion Strings | 68

Green Vegetable Soup with Pistou | 70

Kale, Potato, Tofu, and Sun-Dried Tomato Soup | 73

Provençal Tomato-Fennel Soup with Saffron | 74

Chunky Leek, Potato, and Tomato Soup | 76

Spicy Roasted Tomato–Red Pepper Soup with Salted Basil Cream | 77

Rainy Day Tomato Bisque with Mini Cheese Triangles | 79

Miso Soup with Tofu, Shiitakes, Bok Choy, and Soba Noodles | 81

Nonna's Rice and Potato Soup | 84

Wild Mushroom Soup | 87

Spiced Rutabaga-Apple Soup | 88

Creamy Onion, Leek, and Shallot Bisque | 90

Mom's Minestrone | 93

"Silk Purse" Roasted Leftover Root Vegetable Soup | 95

Turkish Eggplant Soup | 96

Thai Carrot-Ginger Soup | 100

Finnish Jerusalem Artichoke Soup with Marinated Tofu | 103

BUTTERNUT SQUASH SOUP WITH MOLE AND PEPPERS

This full-bodied soup marries butternut squash, bell peppers, and mole sauce, one of Mexico's culinary gifts to the world. It's a favorite cold-weather lunch or simple supper that's rich in texture and flavor. There can be upward of twenty or thirty ingredients in mole, which is why buying it makes sense, especially if you buy an artisanal product from Mexico (see the sidebar). You might add diced avocado as a garnish, as well.

1 medium butternut squash, diced (4 cups)

1½ tablespoons canola or other vegetable oil

1 small onion, finely chopped (⅓ cup)

1 large clove garlic, minced

2 cups chicken or vegetable stock

1½ tablespoons prepared dark mole paste

½ medium red pepper, finely chopped (¼ cup)

½ medium green pepper, finely chopped (¼ cup)

1 teaspoon ground coriander

1 teaspoon ground cumin

Salt and freshly ground black pepper

Sour cream or plain yogurt for garnish

Chopped cilantro leaves for garnish

Sliced scallions for garnish

Preheat the oven to 350 degrees F. Line a baking sheet with aluminum foil.

Toss the squash with a little oil and place on the baking sheet. Bake until soft, 35–40 minutes, turning occasionally. Transfer the squash to a bowl and mash with a fork until more or less smooth. You should have about 1 cup of squash.

In a medium-size saucepan, heat the remaining oil over medium heat. Add the onion and sauté until translucent, about 3 minutes. Add the garlic and cook for 30 seconds. Add the stock, peppers, mole paste, coriander, cumin, and squash and bring to a boil, stirring to blend the mole in the liquid. Reduce the heat to medium and simmer until the peppers are tender, about 6–7 minutes longer. Season to taste with salt and plenty of pepper.

For a decorative garnish, fill a clean plastic squeeze bottle with the sour cream or yogurt. Ladle the soup into two wide, heated bowls. Squeeze the sour cream or yogurt onto the soup in a crosshatch or squiggle pattern, or simply add a dollop of sour cream in the center and sprinkle on the cilantro and scallions. Serve hot or at room temperature.

Mole Choices

If you don't have the time or inclination to make mole, check Hispanic markets and online at sites like www.vivaoaxacafolkart.com, one I particularly like. Some restaurants even sell their own homemade sauce.

Because some mass market brands of mole seem to be thickened with a lot of breadcrumbs, I sometimes add briefly heated ground coriander, cumin, chile powder, and pulverized blanched toasted almonds or pumpkin seeds, or even almond butter to the paste, then purée the mixture and strain it to make commercial products more authentic tasting. If the paste is very stiff, I might dilute it with stock before adding it to the other ingredients to help thin it out.

CARROT-GINGER SOUP WITH CHÈVRE

This perfectly smooth, vibrant orange soup is made with just a few ingredients, so use the best young carrots, high-quality butter, and flavorful stock. (If your carrots are old, you could add a touch of sugar to the soup while cooking.) I frequently add a slice of goat cheese on top of the soup before serving it, but it's delicious alone.

1½ tablespoons unsalted butter

½ pound baby carrots, sliced
(2 cups)

3 tablespoons finely chopped
shallots

2 tablespoons finely chopped
candied ginger

1 tablespoon white rice flour
(see note)

2 cups chicken or vegetable stock

Salt and white pepper

1½ tablespoons snipped fresh
chives, and a few more for garnish

2 (½-inch-thick) slices goat
cheese from a 1½-inch-wide log
(optional)

In a medium-size saucepan, melt the butter over medium heat. Stir in the carrots, shallots, ginger, and rice flour. Cover tightly and sweat over medium-low heat until the carrots are very tender, 20–30 minutes, stirring occasionally.

Scrape the mixture into the jar of an electric blender, add the stock, and purée until completely smooth. Return it to pan. Season to taste with salt and pepper, stir in the chives, and reheat until hot, adding more stock if needed. Ladle into heated soup bowls, add the goat cheese if using, drizzle on the remaining chives, and serve.

Rice Flour

Rice flour is a useful way to thicken soups and keep them smooth. You can also grind raw rice into a powdery consistency in a spice grinder or clean coffee mill. If you grind the rice yourself, you may want to strain the soup to remove any bits of rice, to be sure it's perfectly smooth.

GREEN BEAN–MUSHROOM SOUP WITH FRIZZLED ONION STRINGS

This soup was inspired by a beloved American dish of the 50s: green bean casserole made with canned cream of mushroom soup and topped with fried canned onions. In this updated version, sautéed aromatic vegetables and cremini mushrooms, blended with stock and a little cream, provide the earthy base for diced green beans showered with crunchy onion strings. They're a far cry from the canned variety and dress up even the most mundane soup. You will have more than enough to snack on.

Frizzled Onion Strings (recipe follows)

⅓ pound thin green beans, trimmed and cut into ½-inch lengths

1 tablespoon canola or other vegetable oil

1 small carrot, finely chopped (¼ cup)

1 small onion, finely chopped (¼ cup)

1 small parsnip, finely chopped (¼ cup)

1½ tablespoons unsalted butter

2 cups chopped baby bella (cremini) mushrooms (6 ounces)

1 clove garlic, minced

1 tablespoon finely chopped flat-leaf parsley

1 teaspoon chopped fresh thyme leaves *or* ¼ teaspoon dried leaves

1¼ cups beef, chicken, or vegetable stock

⅓ cup light cream

1 teaspoon freshly squeezed lemon juice or to taste

Salt and freshly ground black pepper to taste

Prepare the Frizzled Onion Strings up to the final frying. In a medium-size saucepan, cook the green beans in boiling salted water until tender; drain and set aside.

In the same saucepan, heat the oil over medium heat. Stir in the carrot, onion, and parsnip. Cover and sweat over low heat until the vegetables are tender, 10–12 minutes, stirring a couple of times. Uncover, add the butter and mushrooms, and sauté until the mushrooms are lightly browned, about 5 minutes. Stir in the garlic and cook for 30 seconds. Add the parsley, thyme, and half of the stock; stir up any browned bits.

Transfer the mixture to a food processor and pulse until chunky-smooth. Return to the saucepan along with the green beans, remaining stock, cream, and lemon juice. Season with salt and pepper to taste; partially cover and simmer for 10 minutes or until heated through.

Meanwhile, finish the Frizzled Onion Strings. Ladle the soup into two bowls, drizzle on some onion strings, and serve.

Frizzled Onion Strings

1 small yellow onion, cut in half horizontally, then into ⅛-inch slices, and separated

¾ cup buttermilk or low-fat milk

½ cup all-purpose flour

¼ cup coarse cornmeal

1 scant teaspoon salt

½ cup canola or other vegetable oil

In a resealable plastic bag, combine the onion and buttermilk and soak for 30 minutes.

In a shallow dish, combine the flour, cornmeal, and salt. Line a plate or baking pan with paper towels.

In a small skillet, heat the oil over medium-high heat to 350 degrees F. on an instant-read or deep-fat frying thermometer. Working in small batches, toss the onion strings in the flour mixture, patting to remove excess flour. Immediately drop them into the oil and cook until golden brown, 1–2 minutes, turning often. With a slotted spoon, remove to the paper towels until all of the onion is cooked. Add additional salt to taste, if desired.

Baby Bella or Cremini Mushrooms

Called both "cremini" and "baby bellas," these light brown mushrooms resemble a darker version of the common white button mushrooms but are more flavorful and somewhat firmer in texture. They're a smaller, younger version of portobello mushrooms; unlike mature portobellos, their underside gills should not be exposed or opened. Wipe and trim before using.

GREEN VEGETABLE SOUP WITH PISTOU

Don't be fooled by this soup, says Karen Berk, a terrific cook and dear friend. Alone, it's bland (dare I say boring). But it's based on an old Provençal recipe and is far more than the sum of its parts. The linchpin is the pistou, the French version of pesto that pulls all the ingredients together. It's very garlicky. You can buy terrific prepared pesto today and add more garlic if you like. As befits foods from the south of France, this soup is delightful at room temperature but may also be served warm.

1 tablespoon fragrant extra-virgin olive oil

1 large zucchini, sliced (1 cup)

Half medium onion, sliced (½ cup)

2 cups chicken stock

⅔ cup frozen shelled edamame or baby lima beans, defrosted

⅓ cup frozen baby peas, defrosted

Salt and freshly ground black pepper

Pistou (recipe follows)

Sour cream, crème fraîche, or plain Greek yogurt for garnish (optional)

In a medium-size saucepan, heat the oil over medium heat. Add the zucchini and onion and sauté until softened, about 10 minutes. Add the chicken stock and bring to a boil. Add the edamame or lima beans and the peas. When the mixture returns to a boil, reduce the heat, and simmer until the vegetables are soft, 5–7 minutes. Let the soup cool, then purée it in the jar of an electric blender. Season to taste with salt and pepper.

Meanwhile, make the pistou.

If you're serving the soup warm, return it to the saucepan and simmer over low heat, making sure it doesn't boil. Serve with a generous dollop of pesto and sour cream or yogurt on top.

Pistou

Makes about ½ cup

1 tablespoon minced garlic (or 1½ tablespoons if you're very brave)

¾ cup chopped flat-leaf parsley

¼ cup chopped basil

2 tablespoons pine nuts or pistachios, toasted

1½ tablespoons extra-virgin olive oil

¼ teaspoon salt

½ cup freshly grated Parmigiano-Reggiano

In a food processor, pulse the garlic, parsley, basil, pine nuts, salt, and olive oil until almost smooth. Add the cheese and briefly blend again. Scrape into a small bowl. Stored in a covered jar in the refrigerator; it will last for at least a week.

KALE, POTATO, TOFU, AND SUN-DRIED TOMATO SOUP

This silky smooth, creamy soup is rich and satisfying but has not a drop of dairy. Puréed tofu and soy milk are the secrets. For the kale, I prefer the lacinato variety, also known as Tuscan, black, or dinosaur kale. I like its full flavor and find it easier to remove the stems and center ribs and to julienne it.

2 tablespoons extra-virgin olive oil

1 medium onion, chopped (½ cup)

1 large clove garlic, minced

2½ cups very flavorful vegetable or chicken stock

1 medium-small Yukon Gold potato, diced (¾ cup)

½ cup diced firm tofu

⅓ cup soy milk

Salt and pepper

Pinch ground cayenne pepper

3 cups loosely packed julienned kale leaves with coarse stems removed

¼ cup finely chopped oil-packed sun-dried tomatoes

In a medium-size saucepan, heat 1 tablespoon of the oil over medium heat. Add the onion and sauté until golden, about 5 minutes. Stir in the garlic and cook for 30 seconds. Add 1½ cups of the stock and the potatoes, partially cover, and gently boil until the potato is tender when pierced with the tip of a knife, about 15 minutes.

Meanwhile, in the jar of an electric blender, purée the tofu and soy milk until smooth, scraping down the sides as needed. Add the potato, onion, and liquid and purée until smooth. Return the soup to the pan and season to taste with salt, pepper, and cayenne. Heat to just below a boil. Do *not* boil. Stir in the kale and tomatoes and simmer until the kale is tender, about 5 minutes. Stir in the remaining olive oil and serve.

PROVENÇAL TOMATO-FENNEL SOUP WITH SAFFRON

Fennel simmered with ripe summer tomatoes in a broth seasoned with thyme and herbes de Provence (see the sidebar), orange zest, and saffron reminds me of sunny days in Provence in southern Franced. A splash of anise-flavored Pernod brightens the taste. If you make the Morello Cherry Soup with Candied Ginger and Fennel on page 36, this is a good place to use the other half of the fennel bulb.

1 tablespoon fragrant extra-virgin olive oil

1½ fennel bulbs, thinly sliced (2 cups)

1 small onion, thinly sliced (½ cup)

2 cloves garlic, thinly sliced

2–3 vine-ripened tomatoes, seeded and coarsely chopped (1½ cups)

1½ cups vegetable or chicken stock

1 sprig fresh thyme

½ teaspoon herbes de Provence or fresh rosemary and dried oregano (see the sidebar)

Grated zest of 1 small orange

Generous pinch saffron

Salt and freshly ground black pepper

2–3 teaspoons Pernod or other anise-flavored liqueur (optional)

2 tablespoons julienned basil or Salted Basil Cream on page 77

In a medium-size saucepan, heat the oil over medium heat. Add the fennel, onion, and garlic; cover and sweat over medium-low heat until tender, 9–10 minutes, stirring occasionally.

Add the tomatoes, 1 cup of the stock, the thyme, herbes de Provence, orange zest, and saffron. Cover and gently boil until the tomatoes are tender and breaking down, about 10 minutes.

Remove the thyme sprig, scrape the soup into a food processor, and pulse until chunky-smooth.

To make the basil cream, add the cream to a small bowl with a pinch of salt and whisk it into soft peaks; then whisk in the basil.

Return the mixture to the saucepan, add the remaining stock, and season to taste with salt and pepper. Bring the soup to a gentle boil and add the Pernod if using. Ladle into bowls, garnish with basil, and serve.

Herbes de Provence

For decades, whenever I visited Provence, I saw small terra-cotta containers filled with a mixture of dried herbs such as savory, rosemary, oregano, and thyme being sold. Some included dried lavender leaves, as well. The first one I bought, tied with raffia and dried flowers, was ridiculously huge. In spite of wrapping a lot of clothes around the pot before putting it in my suitcase, it broke, and my clothes were liberally scented for a long time afterward. It taught me a valuable lesson: Don't buy a large container of something you will only use occasionally before it loses its pungency, unless you just want it for decoration.

If you don't want to buy herbes de Provence, you could add a sprig of fresh rosemary and a little dried oregano or marjoram along with the fresh thyme in the recipe.

CHUNKY LEEK, POTATO, AND TOMATO SOUP

This chunky-smooth soup is so full of flavor and satisfying textures, while still light and simple to make, you can enjoy it at almost any time of the year. To mash the potatoes, I find that an old-fashioned potato masher or fork, rather than a food processor, produces a nicer texture. For a heartier soup, you might add a couple slices of chopped bacon or small cubes of prosciutto during the cooking.

1 tablespoon fragrant extra-virgin olive oil, plus 1 tablespoon to drizzle on before serving

1 large leek, well rinsed, cut in half lengthwise and thinly sliced (¾ cup)

1 small carrot, finely diced (¼ cup)

½ medium celery rib, finely diced (¼ cup)

1 clove garlic, minced

2 cups chicken or vegetable stock

1 medium Yukon Gold potato, finely chopped (1 cup)

¼ cup canned petite diced tomatoes, drained

1 teaspoon finely minced fresh rosemary leaves *or* ¼ teaspoon crushed dried leaves

Salt and freshly ground black pepper

1 tablespoon finely chopped flat-leaf parsley for garnish

In a medium-size saucepan, heat the oil over medium heat. Add the leek, carrot, and celery and sauté until lightly colored, 3–4 minutes, stirring often. Add the garlic and cook for 30 seconds. Pour in the stock, stirring up any browned cooking bits.

Add the potato, cover, and gently boil until tender, about 15 minutes. Stir in the tomatoes, rosemary, and salt and pepper to taste. Using a potato masher, mash the potatoes until chunky-smooth—or transfer to a food processor and pulse until chunky-smooth.

Ladle the soup into two large shallow bowls, add the parsley in the middle, and drizzle the remaining oil in a circle around it.

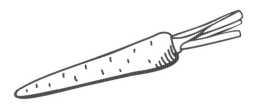

SPICY ROASTED TOMATO-RED PEPPER SOUP WITH SALTED BASIL CREAM

Flame-roasted bell peppers combined with fire-roasted canned tomatoes, sautéed onion, and garlic make this soup addictive. Lightly salted, softly whipped basil cream is a nice garnish to complement the soup's flavors.

1 large red bell pepper

1 tablespoon extra-virgin olive oil

1 small onion, thinly sliced (½ cup)

1 small carrot, thinly sliced (¼ cup)

2 cloves garlic, thinly sliced

1 (14½-ounce) can crushed or diced fire-roasted tomatoes

1 cup vegetable stock

1 teaspoon sugar

¼ teaspoon red pepper flakes

Salt and white pepper

¼ cup heavy cream (optional)

8 basil leaves, chopped

Croutons for garnish (optional)

On top of a gas stove, place the pepper on the burner, close to the flame, and roast until all sides are charred, using tongs to turn it often. Remove, put it in a paper bag, and fold to close tightly (or put it into a bowl and cover with plastic wrap); let it steam until cool. Wipe off the charred skin with paper towels, remove the seeds and membranes, coarsely chop, and set aside.

In a medium-size saucepan, heat the oil over medium heat. Add the onion, carrot, and garlic; cover the pan and sweat over low heat until tender, about 7 minutes, stirring occasionally. Uncover and cook 2–3 minutes longer, until the onion is golden, stirring often. Scrape into a food processor along with the tomatoes and red pepper, and pulse until chunky-smooth or completely smooth.

Return the soup to the saucepan and stir in the stock, sugar, red pepper flakes, and salt and pepper to taste; simmer for 10 minutes.

To make the basil cream, add the cream to a small bowl with a pinch of salt and whisk it into soft peaks; then whisk in the basil.

Taste to adjust the seasonings in the soup, adding more stock if needed. Ladle it into two bowls, add a dollop of the salted basil cream, some croutons, and serve.

RAINY DAY TOMATO BISQUE WITH
MINI CHEESE TRIANGLES

When I was growing up, tomato soup with grilled cheese sandwiches was my family's go-to staple for lunch, especially on gloomy days. Tomato bisque was "fancier," and I grew to love that creamy version. The small grilled cheese triangles are so perfect with the soup, you may want to double the recipe.

Mini Cheese Triangles:

2 slices firm, thin-sliced white bread

2 tablespoons unsalted butter at room temperature

½ teaspoon Dijon mustard

¾ cup shredded sharp or medium Cheddar cheese

Tomato Bisque:

2 tablespoons unsalted butter

1 small onion, finely chopped (⅓ cup)

½ medium celery rib, finely chopped (¼ cup)

2 cloves garlic, finely chopped

1 (14½-ounce) can petite diced tomatoes, fire-roasted, if available

1¼ cups chicken or vegetable stock

2 teaspoons sugar

½ teaspoon dried oregano

⅓ cup heavy or light cream

Salt and white pepper

For the Mini Cheese Triangles: Lightly butter both sides of the bread. Spread a little Dijon mustard on one side of each slice. Set aside.

For the Tomato Bisque: In a medium-size saucepan, melt the butter over medium heat. Stir in the onion and celery and sauté until they start to color, about 5 minutes. Add the garlic and cook for 30 seconds.

Remove about ¼ cup of the diced tomatoes from the can and set aside. Stir in the remaining tomatoes, the stock, sugar, and oregano and gently boil until the vegetables are soft, 12–15 minutes.

While the soup cooks, lightly spray a nonstick skillet with vegetable spray. Heat the skillet over medium heat. Lay 1 slice of bread with the mustard-coated side up in the skillet and sprinkle on the cheese. Cover with the second slice of bread with the mustard on the inside. Cook until the bottom slice is golden brown, about 2 minutes, turn, and cook the second side until golden. Remove, cut off the crusts, and slice diagonally into four triangles.

Scrape the soup into the jar of an electric blender and purée until totally smooth. Return it to the saucepan, stir in the cream and reserved tomatoes, and bring just to a simmer. Season to taste with salt and pepper, ladle into bowls, and serve with the Mini Cheese Triangles.

MISO SOUP WITH TOFU, SHIITAKES, BOK CHOY, AND SOBA NOODLES

This simple, flavorful broth with vegetables, mushrooms, tofu, and udon noodles takes little time to make and is very soothing. Cooked and packaged fresh noodles are available in many markets. They can be simmered in water for a couple of minutes or even microwaved to speed up the short process. To make this a little spicy, add red chile sauce to taste.

½ cup cooked thick udon noodles

1 teaspoon yellow or red miso paste (see the sidebar)

2½ cups water

2–3 teaspoons soy sauce

2 thin slices fresh ginger root, peeled and cut into thin matchsticks

1 clove garlic, thinly sliced crosswise

1 small baby bok choy, cut into ¼-inch slices

3 large shiitake mushrooms, stems removed, wiped, and thickly sliced

1 scallion, white and light green parts, thinly sliced, plus additional slices for garnish

½ cup firm tofu cut into ½-inch cubes

Red chile sauce (optional)

Cook or heat the noodles, drain, and set aside.

Meanwhile, in a small bowl, stir the miso and ½ cup of the water together and set aside.

In a medium-size saucepan, bring the remaining water, 2 teaspoons of the soy sauce, the ginger, and garlic to a boil. Reduce the heat and simmer for 10 minutes.

Add the bok choy, shiitakes, scallion, tofu, and cooked noodles and simmer until the vegetables are wilted, 2–3 minutes. Stir in the diluted miso, add the remaining soy sauce and chile sauce if desired, and heat through. Do not boil. Ladle into bowls and serve with a few slices of scallion sprinkled on the soup.

Miso Paste in Different Colors

Miso pastes have become more available in mainstream supermarkets' deli or dairy departments. As to which one you should buy, the answer is dependent on your own taste. All miso is made from fermented soybeans combined with other ingredients, typically grains. The mildest-tasting pastes range from white to light beige, and the beans are fermented with rice. Yellowish to pale caramel color miso comes from soybeans usually fermented with barley. It has the widest use in general cooking. Red miso is the strongest miso paste generally available, and the beans in it are fermented longer with grains like barley. It can easily overwhelm subtle flavors.

NONNA'S RICE AND POTATO SOUP

Chef Lidia Bastianich says this is the soup her grandmother made most often, and it's still among Lidia's favorites. She says the secret to the rich, complex flavor comes from the rinds of Grana Padano or Parmigiano-Reggiano. When you've finished grating the cheese, wrap the rinds in plastic and keep them in the freezer until you're ready to toss them into a soup. (I also use rinds in Mom's Minestrone on page 93.)

1 tablespoon fragrant extra-virgin olive oil

1 Idaho baking potato, peeled, cut into ½-inch cubes (2 cups)

1 large carrot, peeled and shredded (⅓ cup)

1 medium celery rib, diced (⅓ cup)

Salt

1 scant teaspoon tomato paste

3 cups hot water

1 small bay leaf

Rind of Grana Padano or Parmigiano-Reggiano, scraped and rinsed

Salt and freshly ground black pepper

¼ cup long-grain rice

2 tablespoons freshly grated Grana Padano or Parmigiano-Reggiano

In a medium-size saucepan, heat the oil over medium heat. Add the potato and cook, stirring occasionally, until lightly browned, about 5 minutes. (It's fine if the potatoes stick; just adjust the level of heat to prevent the bits of potato that stick from getting too dark.)

Using a wooden spoon, stir in the carrots and celery and cook until the carrots are softened, 2–3 minutes, and season lightly with salt. Stir in the tomato paste to coat the vegetables. Pour in the hot water, add the bay leaf, and bring the liquid to a boil, scraping up any bits of stuck potato.

Add the cheese rind, lower the heat to maintain a simmer, and season lightly with salt and pepper. Cover and cook until the potatoes begin to fall apart, about 40 minutes.

Stir in the rice and simmer until the rice is tender but still firm, about 12 minutes, stirring often. Remove the bay leaf. Sprinkle with the grated cheese, taste for salt and pepper, ladle into bowls, and serve with additional cheese at the table if desired.

WILD MUSHROOM SOUP

Chef Joy Strang's soup is full of earthy, lush flavors and is pure indulgence. It's a special soup for a winter's celebration.

3–4 portobello mushrooms, including stems, wiped

5 cups water

2 tablespoons canola or other vegetable oil

½ pound wild mushrooms, such as oyster and shiitake, sliced (2 cups)

1 medium shallot, finely diced

1 large clove garlic, minced

1¼ cups hard cider

¾ cup diced dried apples

1 cup heavy cream

Salt and freshly ground black pepper

2 tablespoons coarsely chopped toasted hazelnuts for garnish

In a medium-size pot, combine the portobellos and water and simmer for 1 hour, then strain and discard the solids. Makes 1 cup liquid. The stock may be made ahead of time and stored.

In a medium-size saucepan, heat 1 tablespoon of the oil over medium-high heat. Add the wild mushrooms and cook until browned, 6–7 minutes, stirring often. Add the remaining tablespoon of oil, the shallot and garlic, and cook until they start to brown, about 30 seconds.

Stir in the apple cider, scraping up all the brown cooking bits from the bottom of the pan. Add the dried apples, simmer for 3–4 minutes, and stir in the reserved mushroom stock and heavy cream. Simmer for about 5 minutes. Transfer the mixture to a food processor, and pulse until slightly chunky-smooth.

Return the soup to the pan, season to taste with salt and pepper, heat until hot over medium-high heat, and serve with the hazelnuts sprinkled on top.

SPICED RUTABAGA-APPLE SOUP

In northern Europe, rutabagas mashed with a little butter are familiar autumn fare and are known by several names (see the sidebar). Although considered too earthy tasting by many Americans, when slowly roasted the root becomes quite mild and sweet. In this robust, complex-tasting soup, it's cooked with apple and garam masala, a spice blend typically used in Indian cooking that includes cardamom, cinnamon, clove, cumin, and peppercorns. As garnishes, thinly sliced apple, cilantro, and walnut pieces add visual appeal and texture.

1½ teaspoons canola or other vegetable oil

1 very small onion or ½ medium onion, chopped (¼ cup)

1 clove garlic, minced

2 teaspoons finely chopped fresh ginger

1½–2 teaspoons garam masala

1 flavorful tart-sweet apple, such as Braeburn, peeled and cored

1½ teaspoons unsalted butter

1¾ cups diced rutabaga (see the sidebar for peeling instructions)

2 cups vegetable stock

½ cup half-and-half or light cream

Salt and white pepper

1 tablespoon chopped toasted walnuts

½ tablespoon chopped cilantro

In a medium-size saucepan, heat the oil over medium heat. Add the onion and gently sauté until it's translucent and lightly browned, about 5 minutes, stirring occasionally. Add the garlic, ginger, and 1½ teaspoons garam masala and cook for 1 minute longer, stirring a couple of times.

Dice about half the apple, and reserve the rest for the garnish. Add the butter, rutabaga, and diced apple, turning to coat them well. Cook for 2 minutes, pour in the stock, and bring to a boil. Reduce the heat to a simmer, cover, and cook until the rutabaga is tender when pierced with a knife, 35–40 minutes.

Transfer the mixture to the jar of an electric blender or food processor and purée until smooth. Return to the pan, stir in the half-and-half, the remaining garam masala if desired, and season to taste with salt and pepper. Heat until hot. Ladle the soup into bowls. Add the walnuts, apple slices, and cilantro and serve.

A Rutabaga by Any Other Name

In northern Europe, rutabagas are far more popular than they are here, although they go by different names. The Irish call them turnips, the English call them swedes, and in Scotland they are sometimes known as neeps.

Whatever you call them, rutabagas are generally quite large and hard to peel and cut up. Some markets sell them already diced. If you have a whole one, take a sharp knife, place the rutabaga on its flat end, and cut it in half. Turn it on the cut side and cut it into ¾-inch slices, discarding the ends. Using a paring knife, cut off the tough skin and cut the flesh into ¾-inch cubes. Use extra rutabaga in "Silk Purse" Roasted Leftover Root Vegetable Soup (page 95).

CREAMY ONION, LEEK, AND SHALLOT BISQUE

This is a soup for onion lovers. Caramelized onions, leeks, and shallots (or only onions if you prefer) are puréed with chicken stock and then combined with sherry, sautéed onion, and a splash of cream at the end. What makes it so delicious are the fried leeks—and the Gruyère crostini, a contemporary interpretation of the typical (and often too heavy) cheese topping on many onion soups. Pass any extras at the table. They're yummy!

2½ tablespoons unsalted butter

4 medium onions, thinly sliced (3 cups)

3 medium leeks, well washed, cut in half lengthwise and thinly sliced (1½ cups)

1 cup thinly sliced shallots

⅓ cup medium sherry, such as Amontillado

1 teaspoon chopped fresh tarragon leaves

2 cups chicken or vegetable stock

¼ cup heavy or light cream

Coarse sea salt and white pepper

4–6 thin slices French baguette, lightly toasted

1 clove garlic, cut in half

2 tablespoons olive oil

½ cup finely shredded Gruyère or Swiss cheese

In a medium-size saucepan, melt 2 tablespoons of the butter over medium heat. Add 2 cups of the onions, 1 cup of the leeks, and shallots and sauté until soft and golden brown, about 8 minutes. Stir and scrape the pan often to prevent burning.

Meanwhile, in a small skillet, heat the remaining ½ tablespoon of butter over medium heat. Add the remaining cup of onion and sauté until soft and rich golden brown, 7–9 minutes, stirring often. Watch that they don't burn. Set aside.

Prepare the Crunchy Leek Topping (see next page).

Pour the sherry into the saucepan with the leeks and shallots and bring to a boil over high heat, stirring up all the browned bits. Scrape the mixture into the jar of an electric blender or food processor, add the tarragon, and purée until smooth. Return the mixture to the saucepan, add the stock and cream; simmer for 5 minutes. Stir in the caramelized onion from the small skillet, season to taste with salt and pepper, and keep warm over medium-low heat.

For the crostini: Rub the toasted bread with garlic and brush with oil. Lay the slices on a cookie sheet or on the tray of a toaster oven, sprinkle on the cheese, and broil until the cheese is melted and lightly browned. Ladle the soup into two wide bowls, sprinkle on the leeks, add 2 crostini to each bowl, and serve at once.

Crunchy Leek Topping

What a perfect use for the darker green parts of leeks—but not the very ends. For slicing leeks very thin, I love my OXO hand-held mandolin slicer, set on the narrowest setting, about 1⁄16 inch. You can also slice the leek by hand. The oil, once strained, may be reused for frying.

Canola or other vegetable oil for frying

1⁄2 cup well-rinsed and very thinly sliced darker green parts of leeks, reserved from the soup

In a small, deep saucepan, pour in enough oil to measure 1 inch deep; heat over medium-high heat until the oil registers 350 degrees F. on a deep-fat frying thermometer.

Set a small strainer over a large glass measuring cup. Line a bowl with paper towels.

When the oil is hot, add the leeks and cook until lightly browned and crisp, about 1 minute, stirring constantly. Immediately remove the pan from the heat and pour the leeks into the strainer. Transfer to paper towels to drain. Strain the oil and reserve for other purposes.

MOM'S MINESTRONE

While living and traveling in Italy, I ate countless bowls of minestrone. They varied widely, but I usually found them comforting. Puréed white beans added to the stock make my minestrone heartier than those with a thin broth. The mix of vegetables is only my suggestion. It changes according to what's in my refrigerator.

If you have the rind of a piece of Grana Padano or Parmigiano-Reggiano, do as Lidia Bastianich does with her Nonna's Rice and Potato Soup on page 84: add it to the soup while it simmers. For those who love pasta in their minestrone, cook it first and add it close to serving time to keep it from absorbing too much of the liquid.

1 tablespoon fragrant extra-virgin olive oil, plus additional oil to drizzle on the soup before serving

1 medium onion, finely diced (½ cup)

1 medium carrot, finely diced (⅓ cup)

1 medium celery rib, finely diced (⅓ cup)

2 large cloves garlic, minced

2 cups stock (I prefer half chicken and half beef), divided

1 baby bok choy, cut crosswise into ½-inch slices

½ cup rinsed and drained canned cannellini beans

¼ pound white mushrooms, sliced (½ cup)

1 small zucchini, sliced (⅓ cup)

⅓ cup drained canned diced tomatoes

1 tablespoon tomato paste

½ teaspoon dried oregano

⅓ cup drained canned garbanzo beans

Rind of Grana Padano or Parmigiano-Reggiano rind (optional)

2 tablespoons chopped flat-leaf parsley

Salt and freshly ground black pepper

Grated Parmigiano-Reggiano

In a medium-size saucepan, heat the oil over medium heat. Stir in the onion, carrot, and celery; cover and sweat until softened, about 5 minutes, stirring occasionally. Stir in the garlic, cook for 30 seconds, then add 1½ cups of leftover stock and the bok choy and gently boil for 8 minutes.

Meanwhile, in a food processor, combine the remaining ½ cup of stock with the cannellini beans and purée until smooth. Add them along with the mushrooms, zucchini, tomatoes, tomato paste, oregano, and garbanzo beans to the saucepan along with the Grana Padano or Parmigiano-Reggiano rind, if using; partially cover and gently boil for 25 minutes. Stir in the parsley and season to taste with salt and pepper. Ladle into bowls, add grated Parmigiano-Reggiano on top, drizzle on a little olive oil, and serve.

"SILK PURSE" ROASTED LEFTOVER ROOT VEGETABLE SOUP

How many orphaned carrots, flabby turnips, or homely parsnips have you found in your refrigerator? This hearty soup is one way to turn those less than pristine vegetables into a tasty "silk purse." You can make the soup more exotic by adding ras al hanout, a warming mixture of ground spices typically found in Morocco (see the sidebar). Use whatever roots you have, including butternut squash, rutabagas, celery root, and those listed below.

2 tablespoons fragrant extra-virgin olive oil

1 small onion, diced (¼ cup)

2 large cloves garlic, chopped

1 tablespoon *ras al hanout* (optional)

2 cups mixed root vegetables, such as carrot, celery, fennel, parsnips, and turnip, cut into ½-inch cubes

Salt

Pinch cayenne pepper

2–2½ cups vegetable stock

⅓ cup canned chickpeas, rinsed and drained

1 teaspoon finely grated fresh ginger root

½ small jalapeño, or other chile pepper, seeds removed and finely chopped (optional)

¼ cup pitted, oil-cured, black olives, coarsely chopped (optional)

2 tablespoons chopped cilantro leaves

In a medium-size saucepan, heat 1 tablespoon of the oil over medium-low heat. Add the onion and sauté until softened and starting to color, about 5 minutes, stirring often. Stir in the garlic and ras al hanout if using, and cook for 30 seconds. Add the remaining oil and root vegetables, turning to coat them evenly.

Season the mixture with ½ teaspoon of salt or to taste and the cayenne; partially cover the pan and sweat the vegetables until lightly caramelized and almost soft, 10–15 minutes, stirring occasionally.

Add 2 cups of the vegetable stock, the chickpeas, ginger root, and jalapeño if using; simmer until the vegetables are completely tender, about 10 minutes, adding additional stock if needed. Stir in the olives, ladle into bowls, sprinkle on the cilantro, and serve.

Ras al Hanout

This Moroccan spice blend typically includes chile peppers, coriander, cardamom, cumin, clove, nutmeg, and turmeric. The name means "head of the shop" and suggests it's the best the spice seller has to offer. While I was shopping at an herb vendor in Marrakech's Jemaa El Fna square, the owner offered me a bag of his. It was so fragrant and far from the mucty, faded seasoning I'd tasted in many commercial products. You can buy it online and in many markets, but shop where the turnover is brisk for the freshest flavors.

TURKISH EGGPLANT SOUP

During the Ottoman Empire, the sultan's cooks at Topkapi Palace prepared eggplants in countless ways. The fruit (yes—it has seeds) is still beloved in Turkey. This soup is based on Imam Bayildi, a very popular room-temperature meze, or appetizer. The name means the imam, or holy man, fainted. History doesn't tell us whether such a dramatic result was caused by the sheer joy of the dish's beauty and taste or by the lavish use of the then costly olive oil. The dish is in a category of vegetables slowly braised in olive oil, known as zeytinyaglis. As a soup, it may be served either at room temperature or warm.

½ medium eggplant, American, Italian, or Japanese variety (6–7 ounces)

Salt

3 tablespoons fragrant extra-virgin olive oil

1 medium onion, thinly sliced (⅔ cup)

2 large cloves garlic, finely chopped

1 plum tomato, cored, seeded, and chopped

3 tablespoons finely chopped flat-leaf parsley

1 teaspoon fresh thyme leaves *or* ¼ teaspoon dried

1¾ cups vegetable or chicken stock

1 tablespoon tomato paste

1 teaspoon freshly squeezed lemon juice

¾–1 teaspoon sugar

Salt and freshly ground black pepper

1 tablespoon julienned fresh mint leaves *or* 1 teaspoon dried leaves (added with the stock)

2 tablespoons crumbled feta for garnish (optional)

1 tablespoon pine nuts for garnish

Peel the eggplant; slice it in half lengthwise and then crosswise into ¼-inch slices. Put the slices in a large strainer or colander, sprinkle with a teaspoon of salt, toss, and set aside to drain for 20–30 minutes. Rinse under cold water and pat dry with paper towels.

In a medium-size saucepan, heat half of the oil over medium-low heat. Add the onion and sauté until wilted and lightly colored, 3–4 minutes, stirring occasionally. Pour in the remaining oil, stir in the garlic, eggplant, tomatoes, parsley, and thyme; cover and cook over low heat until the eggplant is easily broken into small pieces with a wooden spatula or spoon, about 15 minutes, stirring a couple of times.

Add the stock, tomato paste, lemon juice, and sugar. If you're using dried mint leaves, add them here. Season to taste with salt and plenty of freshly ground black pepper and simmer for 10 minutes. Taste to adjust the flavors. Let the soup cool to room temperature, if desired. Stir in fresh mint leaves, ladle into bowls, sprinkle on the feta if using, and the pine nuts, and serve.

CURRIED PUMPKIN-COCONUT SOUP

Warmly spicy Malaysian red curry paste enriches this comforting blend of pumpkin and coconut milk. Unsweetened, toasted coconut and minced fresh rosemary stirred in before serving add color and texture. If you make the Black Bean, Pumpkin, and Tomato Soup on page 117, you can use the extra canned pumpkin here. Coconut water is now available in many supermarkets. Coconut oil is also more available than it used to be. See the sidebar to discover some of their benefits.

1 tablespoon coconut or vegetable oil

1 small onion, finely chopped (⅓ cup)

1 clove garlic, finely chopped

1¼ cups vegetable stock

¼–½ teaspoon Thai or Malaysian red curry paste (see the headnote about strength of curry paste, page 157)

1 cup canned or puréed cooked pumpkin

½ cup coconut milk, not "lite" variety

½ teaspoon ground coriander

Salt

¼–½ cup coconut water or additional stock

¼ cup unsweetened shredded coconut

1 teaspoon minced fresh rosemary

In a medium-size saucepan, heat the oil over medium heat. Add the onion and sauté until wilted and lightly colored, about 4 minutes. Stir in the garlic and cook for 30 seconds. Add the stock, curry paste, and pumpkin; bring to a boil, stirring to blend. Scrape into the jar of an electric blender and purée until smooth.

Return the soup to the saucepan. Stir in the coconut milk, coriander, and salt to taste. Return to a simmer and add enough coconut water to achieve the right consistency. Keep warm.

In a small skillet, toast the coconut over medium heat until golden, about 3 minutes, stirring or shaking the pan, and watching that it doesn't burn. Ladle the soup into 2 large soup bowls, sprinkle on the toasted coconut, and the basil, and serve.

Nuts for Coconuts

If you're lactose intolerant or want to add another flavor to your soups, coconut milk is a great replacement for dairy products. You may now be able to find half-gallon containers of coconut milk, which keep for a long time in the refrigerator. Unopened cans last indefinitely on your pantry shelf.

Coconut water is the clear liquid from immature coconuts. Unlike coconut milk, it is very low in fat. Coconut water is becoming more popular because it helps raise electrolytes without all the sugar of many sports drinks. I find it useful for thinning soups, as well.

My choice of a garnish here is toasted, unsweetened sliced or shredded coconut. It's tasty and crispy without adding a lot of sugar.

THAI CARROT-GINGER SOUP

The same combination of carrots and candied ginger used for this smooth and delicious soup are also used for the soup with chèvre on page 67. Here they take flight to Asia with the addition of Thai curry paste and a hint of coconut milk. Rice flour, or rice finely ground in a clean spice mill, thickens the soup into a velvety smooth consistency. The optional addition of shrimp would make it a more substantial meal.

1½ tablespoons coconut oil or unsalted butter

3-4 medium carrots, chopped (2 cups)

3 tablespoons finely chopped shallots

2 tablespoons finely chopped candied ginger

1 tablespoon white rice flour

1½ cups chicken or vegetable stock

½ cup canned coconut milk, not "lite" variety

¼-½ teaspoon Thai red curry paste

10-12 peeled and deveined medium shrimp (optional)

Salt and white pepper

1-1½ teaspoons freshly squeezed lime juice

1 tablespoon finely chopped cilantro leaves or rosemary

In a medium-size saucepan, heat the oil or butter over medium heat. Stir in the carrots, shallots, ginger, and rice flour. Cover tightly and sweat over medium-low heat until the carrots are very tender, 20–30 minutes, stirring occasionally.

Scrape the mixture into the jar of an electric blender, add the stock, and purée until completely smooth. Return the soup to the pan, stir in the coconut milk and curry paste, and bring to a simmer. Add the shrimp, if using, and cook until they are pink and just cooked through. Season to taste with salt and pepper, add the lime juice, ladle into soup bowls, garnish with herbs and serve.

FINNISH JERUSALEM ARTICHOKE SOUP
WITH MARINATED TOFU

Jerusalem artichokes, or sunchokes, impart a subtle, earthy-nutty flavor to this ivory-colored soup. I first tasted it in the kitchen of Jarmo Vähä-Savo, the executive chef of G.W. Sundmans, an elegant, three-Michelin-starred restaurant in Helsinki. Like many contemporary Finnish dishes, it's a simple blend of eclectic ingredients. In this soup, they're accented with tiny cubes of tofu marinated in olive oil and thyme that really make this dish. Serve it hot or at room temperature. I urge you to try it.

¼ cup extra firm tofu, cut into ¼-inch cubes, plus more for garnish

1½ tablespoons fruity extra-virgin olive oil

½ teaspoon fresh thyme leaves

⅛ teaspoon salt

8 ounces Jerusalem artichokes, scrubbed and coarsely chopped

1 small Yukon Gold or other waxy potato, peeled and diced (½ cup)

1 small onion, sliced (⅓ cup)

1¼ cups water

⅓ cup dry white wine

¼ cup heavy or light cream

Salt

In a small bowl, stir the tofu, olive oil, thyme, and ⅛ teaspoon salt together and let marinate for at least 45 minutes.

Meanwhile, in a medium-size saucepan, combine the Jerusalem artichokes, potato, and onion with the water and the wine. Cover and gently boil until the vegetables are tender, about 30 minutes. Transfer the vegetables and liquid to the jar of an electric blender and purée until completely smooth.

Return the purée to the pan, stir in the cream, season to taste with salt, and heat until hot. Ladle the soup into shallow soup bowls, spoon a generous tablespoon of tofu in the center of each, and serve.

LEGUME, NUT, AND BEAN

Lentil Soup with Balsamic-Glazed Butternut Squash and Goat Cheese | 107

Spanish Red Lentil and Chorizo Soup | 108

French Green Lentil Soup | 111

Vegetarian Split Green Pea Soup | 112

Black Bean, Pumpkin, and Tomato Soup | 117

White Bean, Vegetable, and Sun-Dried Tomato Soup | 118

Double Chickpea–Two Tomato Soup | 121

Nanny Annie's Barley-Mushroom Soup | 122

Turkey-Barley and Spinach Soup | 124

Hearty Turkey-Vegetable-Bean Soup | 127

Moroccan Tomato-Chickpea Soup | 128

Broccoli-Almond Soup with Gruyère Crisps | 130

Celery Root, Chestnut, and Gorgonzola Soup | 132

West African Peanut Soup with Chicken | 137

Radish Greens Soup with Toasted Hazelnuts | 139

LENTIL SOUP WITH BALSAMIC-GLAZED BUTTERNUT SQUASH AND GOAT CHEESE

This hearty combination of lentils, butternut squash, and goat cheese is a robust, satisfying meal. While any lentils work, I like shiny, black beluga lentils, said to resemble caviar, because they glisten when cooked and hold their shape better than brown lentils. In general, when cooking lentils and legumes, don't add salt or acidic ingredients until they are tender because it lengthens the cooking time. Since this recipe uses only a cup of squash, you could easily pick up some of the already-diced squash that's now available in many places.

1½ tablespoons fragrant extra-virgin olive oil

1 medium onion, finely chopped (½ cup)

1 large clove garlic, minced

½ cup lentils, preferably black beluga lentils, rinsed under cool water and picked over

4 cups vegetable or chicken stock

1 small bay leaf

1 teaspoon dried thyme leaves

½ teaspoon dried oregano leaves

½ butternut squash, diced (1 cup)

4 teaspoons balsamic vinegar, plus additional vinegar for drizzling at the end

Salt and freshly ground black pepper

¼ cup crumbled goat cheese

1 small scallion, thinly sliced, for garnish

In a medium-size saucepan, heat 1 tablespoon of the olive oil over medium heat. Add the onion and sauté until wilted and lightly colored, about 4 minutes. Add the garlic and cook for 30 seconds, then stir in the lentils, 3 cups of the stock, the bay leaf, thyme, and oregano. Bring the liquid to a boil, cover, and reduce to a simmer; cook until the lentils are completely tender, 25–35 minutes, depending on the variety and freshness of the lentils.

Meanwhile, in a large skillet, heat the remaining ½ tablespoon of oil over medium-high heat. Add the butternut squash and sauté until lightly browned on all sides and just cooked through. Stir in the balsamic vinegar and toss to coat. Season to taste with salt and pepper.

When the lentils are cooked, remove the bay leaf, transfer the mixture to a food processor, and pulse until chunky-smooth. Return the soup to the saucepan, add the squash and the remaining cup of stock. Return the soup to a boil, adjusting the seasonings and vinegar to taste.

Ladle the soup into bowls, sprinkle on the cheese and scallions, and serve.

SPANISH RED LENTIL AND CHORIZO SOUP

On cold nights, my idea of comfort food is often a hearty soup and some crusty bread. A bowl of this thick, flavorful Spanish soup more than meets that standard. Red lentils, spicy chorizo (see the sidebar), and Pimentón de la Vera, Spain's smoky paprika, add up to a mouthful of tastes and textures.

1 tablespoon fragrant extra-virgin olive oil

1 medium onion, diced (½ cup)

1 medium red bell pepper, diced (⅓ cup)

½ medium jalapeño pepper, finely chopped (2 tablespoons)

1 large clove garlic, minced

1 teaspoon ground cumin

2½–3 cups chicken stock

4 ounces Spanish chorizo, casing removed and chopped (1 cup)

½ cup dried red lentils, rinsed under cool water and picked over

2 tablespoons chopped oil-packed, sun-dried tomatoes

Salt and freshly ground black pepper

1 tablespoon chopped fresh mint leaves

2 tablespoons plain Greek-style yogurt

In a medium-size saucepan, heat the oil over medium-high heat. Add the onion, red pepper, and jalapeño and sauté until wilted, 3–4 minutes. Stir in the garlic and cumin, pour in 2½ cups of the stock, and bring to a boil over high heat, stirring up any browned bits.

Add the chorizo, lentils, and tomatoes; cover, reduce the heat to a simmer, and cook until the lentils are tender, 15–20 minutes. Season to taste with salt and pepper. Stir in the remaining stock if the soup is too thick and heat through.

Ladle the soup into two wide bowls. Sprinkle on the mint, add a dollop of yogurt, and serve.

Spanish vs. Mexican Chorizo

Spanish chorizo is already cured when you buy it, so it only needs to be heated. The Mexican version is sold raw and should be removed from the casing before it is cooked through.

FRENCH GREEN LENTIL SOUP

You can make this satisfying soup with any variety of lentils, but French green lentils, or lentilles de Puy, grown in France's Le Puy region, are exceptional. They're smaller in size, green-gray in color, with bluish striated lines. Although they take slightly longer to cook, they hold their shape and add a nice toothsome quality to this soup.

1 tablespoon fragrant extra-virgin olive oil

1 medium leek, well rinsed, cut in half lengthwise, and white and pale green parts thinly sliced (½ cup)

1 small carrot, diced (¼ cup)

½ medium celery rib, diced (¼ cup)

½ yellow or red bell pepper, diced (¼ cup)

1 large clove garlic, finely chopped

2½–3 cups vegetable or chicken stock

¼ cup canned petite diced tomatoes

½ cup green French lentils, rinsed under cool water and picked over

1 bay leaf

1 teaspoon dried thyme leaves

Salt and freshly ground black pepper

½ teaspoon sherry vinegar

2 tablespoons finely chopped mint, plus a little more for garnish

In a medium-size saucepan, heat the oil over medium heat. Stir in the leek and sauté until it begins to wilt, about 2 minutes. Add the carrot, celery, and bell pepper and cook for 2 minutes, stirring often. Add the garlic, cook for 30 seconds, and pour in 2½ cups of the stock, stirring up any browned cooking bits.

Stir in the tomatoes, lentils, bay leaf, and thyme and bring the liquid to a boil over high heat. Cover, reduce the heat so the liquid is simmering, and cook until the lentils are tender, about 50 minutes— 30 minutes for brown lentils—stirring occasionally, adding the remaining stock if needed.

Remove the bay leaf and discard. Season to taste with salt and plenty of black pepper, stir in the sherry vinegar, and return briefly to a boil. Before serving, stir in the mint. Ladle the soup into bowls, sprinkle on the remaining mint, and serve.

VEGETARIAN SPLIT GREEN PEA SOUP

Split green pea soup is another family favorite. When my son Ben and many friends became vegetarian, I came up with this version using vegetable stock and added a "meaty" parsnip in place of the traditional ham. If you prefer meat in your soup, look at the Yellow Split Pea and Sausage Soup recipe on page 210.

1 tablespoon canola or other vegetable oil

1 small carrot, finely chopped (¼ cup)

½ medium celery rib, finely chopped (¼ cup)

½ medium onion, finely chopped (¼ cup)

½ medium parsnip, finely chopped (¼ cup)

⅔ cup green split peas, rinsed under cool water and picked over

1½ cups vegetable stock

1½ cups water

½ teaspoon dried thyme leaves

½ bay leaf

Salt and freshly ground black pepper

Pumpernickel-Parmesan Croutons (recipe follows)

In a medium-size saucepan, heat the oil over medium heat. Stir in the carrot, celery, onion, and parsnip; cover the pan and sweat over medium-low heat until the vegetables are soft, about 10 minutes, stirring occasionally.

Add the peas, stock, half of the water, thyme, bay leaf, and salt and pepper to taste. Bring the mixture to a boil, cover, and reduce the heat so the liquid is simmering. Cook until the peas are very tender, about 1 hour.

Meanwhile, make the Pumpernickel-Parmesan Croutons.

Remove the bay leaf, scrape the mixture into a food processor, and pulse until the soup is chunky-smooth. Return it to the pan and stir in enough of the remaining water to achieve the proper consistency. Heat until hot and serve with croutons if desired.

Pumpernickel-Parmesan Croutons

Unless you really love pumpernickel bread, it makes more sense to buy one pumpernickel bagel, which will be plenty for these croutons. The crunchy cubes can be made ahead and stored in an airtight container for several days. Use extras on salads or other soups.

1 large pumpernickel bagel, crusts removed, cut into ½-inch cubes (2 cups)

½ tablespoon extra-virgin olive oil

1 small clove garlic, minced

Salt and freshly ground pepper

2 tablespoons freshly grated Parmigiano-Reggiano or other flavorful grating cheese

Preheat the oven to 400 degrees F. In a small bowl, combine the bread cubes, oil, garlic, and a little salt and pepper. Spread on a baking sheet and bake until crisp, about 10 minutes, stirring once or twice. Remove, sprinkle on the cheese, toss to coat, and cool.

Chile-Spiced Pumpkin Seeds

These tasty seeds—which I use to add texture and heat to my Black Bean, Pumpkin, and Tomato Soup (recipe follows)— are positively addictive. They're spectacular as a soup garnish and great for cocktail parties.

1 cup raw, hulled pumpkin seeds

1 teaspoon canola or other vegetable oil

2 teaspoons hot or mild chile powder

½ teaspoon ground cumin

½ teaspoon salt

Pinch cayenne pepper (optional)

Preheat the oven to 350 degrees F. Lightly oil a baking sheet.

In a bowl, combine the pumpkin seeds, oil, chile powder, cumin, salt, and cayenne if using. Spread on the baking sheet and bake for 25–30 minutes, turning occasionally. Remove and let cool. Store in an airtight container.

BLACK BEAN, PUMPKIN, AND TOMATO SOUP

This easy-to-make Caribbean-inspired black bean soup (almost everything is from your pantry shelf) blends pumpkin, tomatoes, ham, and sherry wine with the beans for a complex and satisfying meal. It's garnished with a dollop of sour cream and spicy pumpkin seeds instead of croutons. Served with a little glass of sherry—it's a magical pairing.

Chile-Spiced Pumpkin Seeds for garnish (page 115)

1 tablespoon olive oil

1 medium onion, finely chopped (½ cup)

1 large clove garlic, minced

1½ teaspoons ground cumin

1¼ cups beef or chicken stock

¾ cup canned black beans, rinsed and drained

½ cup diced canned tomatoes, drained

½ cup canned pumpkin or mashed cooked fresh pumpkin

½ cup boiled ham, cut into ⅛-inch cubes

1 tablespoon sherry vinegar

Salt and freshly ground black pepper

⅓ cup medium sherry, such as Amontillado

Sour cream or plain Greek yogurt for garnish (optional)

Make the Chile-Spiced Pumpkin Seeds.

In a medium-size saucepan, heat the oil over medium heat. Add the onion and sauté until lightly colored, 4–5 minutes. Add the garlic and cook for 30 seconds. Stir in the cumin and stock and bring to a simmer.

Meanwhile, in a food processor, combine the beans and tomatoes and pulse until the beans have started to smooth but are still somewhat chunky. Scrape into the saucepan and stir in the pumpkin, ham, and vinegar and bring to a boil. Reduce the heat and simmer for 15 minutes.

Season the soup to taste with salt and plenty of black pepper. Stir in the sherry, cook briefly, and ladle the soup into bowls. Top with a dollop of sour cream and Chile-Spiced Pumpkin Seeds if desired.

WHITE BEAN, VEGETABLE, AND SUN-DRIED TOMATO SOUP

This rustic soup reminds me of Tuscany, where cannellini, or white beans, are served in countless ways, including in salads and soups. Here the mild-tasting beans simmer in an aromatic broth of vegetables, garlic, pancetta, and rosemary. Asiago and Rosemary Crostini (recipe follows) are a tempting addition.

1 tablespoon fragrant extra-virgin olive oil, plus additional oil for drizzling

1 small carrot, finely diced (¼ cup),

½ medium celery rib, finely diced (¼ cup)

1 small onion, finely diced (¼ cup)

2 large cloves garlic, finely chopped

¼ cup pancetta, cut in ¼-inch cubes

1½ cups canned cannellini, rinsed and drained (1 15½-ounce can)

2 cups chicken or vegetable stock

1½ teaspoons minced fresh rosemary leaves

½ bay leaf

1½ tablespoons minced oil-packed, sun-dried tomatoes

Salt and freshly ground black pepper

In a medium-size saucepan, heat the oil over medium heat. Add the carrot, celery, and onion; cover the pan and sweat the vegetables until tender, about 7 minutes, stirring occasionally. Uncover, stir in the garlic and cook for 30 seconds; then add the pancetta and cook for 1 minute, stirring often.

Add the cannellini, stock, rosemary, and bay leaf and bring the liquid to a boil. Reduce the heat to a simmer, partially cover, and cook for 15 minutes.

Meanwhile, make the Asiago and Rosemary Crostini, if serving.

Remove the bay leaf from the soup, stir in the sun-dried tomatoes, add salt and pepper to taste, and simmer for 5 more minutes. Ladle the soup into bowls, drizzle on a little olive oil, and serve.

Asiago and Rosemary Crostini

In Tuscany, crostini are little slices of toasted or stale bread spread with a topping and served as hors d'oeuvres or to accompany soups or salads. The rosemary oil–brushed bread with Asiago is one of my favorite combinations. Store any extra oil in a covered jar to drizzle it on other soups as a final garnish.

1 tablespoon rosemary oil (or fragrant extra-virgin olive oil infused with rosemary; see recipe directions)

4 (¼-inch-wide) slices stale, firm-textured bread

1 small clove garlic, split

2 tablespoons grated Asiago cheese

If you do not have rosemary oil, crush or bruise ½ tablespoon fresh rosemary leaves and combine with ½ cup olive oil in a small microwave-safe bowl. Heat in the microwave on medium for 2 minutes. Remove and cool to room temperature.

In a toaster oven, line the baking tray with aluminum foil and turn the temperature to broil. Lightly brush one side of each slice of bread with the oil and rub with garlic. Place the oiled-side up in the baking tray and broil just until lightly browned, about 2 minutes.

Remove the tray from the oven, turn the bread over, brush the second side with oil, rub again with garlic, and sprinkle the grated cheese over the slices. Broil until the cheese is bubbling and golden brown, about 2 minutes more, checking often so they don't burn.

DOUBLE CHICKPEA–TWO TOMATO SOUP

You could describe this creamy vegetarian soup as humble, but it's also full of flavors and colors and takes very little time and effort to make. Puréed canned chickpeas and tomatoes are combined with whole chickpeas, sun-dried tomatoes, and fresh basil. If desired, serve each bowl with a dollop of pesto, either purchased or homemade, or grated Parmesan cheese.

1½ tablespoons fragrant olive oil

1 small onion, finely chopped (⅓ cup)

1 small carrot, finely chopped (¼ cup)

½ medium celery rib (¼ cup)

1 large clove garlic, finely chopped

1½ cups canned garbanzo beans, rinsed and drained

¾ cup canned chopped tomatoes

1¾ cups vegetable stock

¼ cup oil-packed sun-dried tomatoes, blotted on paper towels and finely chopped

Salt and freshly ground black pepper

1½ tablespoons finely chopped fresh basil leaves

Bruce's Homemade Basil Pesto (page 44) *or* grated Parmigiano-Reggiano for garnish

In a medium-size saucepan, heat the oil over medium-high heat. Add the onion, carrot, and celery and sauté until limp and lightly colored, 4–5 minutes. Stir in the garlic and cook for 30 seconds. Add 1 cup of the garbanzos, the canned tomatoes, and ¾ cup of the stock. Cover, lower the heat, and simmer for 15 minutes. Scrape into an electric blender and purée until completely smooth.

Return the soup to the pan, stir in the remaining stock and chickpeas, the sun-dried tomatoes, and season with salt and pepper to taste. Bring the soup to a simmer, add the basil, and taste to adjust the seasonings. Ladle into two bowls. If desired, add a dollop of pesto or a sprinkle of Parmesan cheese.

NANNY ANNIE'S
BARLEY-MUSHROOM SOUP

Bette Shifman says her grandmother's soup was traditionally served when her family broke the fast after Yom Kippur, the Jewish Day of Atonement. She adds, "Nothing in the world could taste as good after not eating for a whole day!" It can be prepared with any kind of stock, including vegetable or mushroom, as a vegan soup. Bette serves it with a rustic, sourdough rye bread.

¼ cup dried porcini, shiitake, or any combination of mushrooms

1 cup boiling water

3 teaspoons olive oil

½ pound fresh cremini or white mushrooms, sliced (1½ cups)

1 large onion, chopped (¾ cup)

1 medium carrot, chopped (½ cup)

1 medium celery rib, chopped (½ cup)

1 large clove garlic, finely chopped

3 cups chicken, beef, vegetable, or mushroom stock

¼ cup pearled barley

¼ teaspoon salt

Freshly ground black pepper

1 tablespoon chopped fresh dill leaves

1 tablespoon chopped flat-leaf parsley

1 teaspoon chopped fresh thyme

In a small bowl, soak the dried mushrooms in the boiling water for about 20 minutes.

Meanwhile, in a heavy skillet, heat 1 teaspoon of the oil over medium heat. Add the fresh mushrooms and cook until golden and reduced by about half, 5–10 minutes., stirring occasionally. (You can skip this step in a pinch, but it adds a lot of flavor.)

Using a coffee filter or strainer lined with a paper towel, strain the soaked, dried mushrooms and reserve the liquid. Chop the dried mushrooms and add them to the fresh mushrooms.

In a medium-size saucepan, heat the remaining 2 teaspoons of olive oil over medium heat until hot. Stir in the onion and sauté until soft, 4–5 minutes. Add the carrots and celery and cook until soft and beginning to caramelize, about 6 minutes.

Stir in garlic, cook for 30 seconds, then add the mushroom mixture and soaking liquid and simmer for 1–2 minutes. Add the stock, barley, salt, and a pinch of pepper. Simmer uncovered until the barley is cooked, about 30 minutes. Stir in the fresh dill, parsley, and thyme and taste to adjust the seasoning. Serve with a rustic, sourdough rye bread.

TURKEY-BARLEY AND SPINACH SOUP

Here's another simple, comforting soup, made with leftover turkey or chicken breast. In this one, the bird is combined with barley and spinach. I find that both kids and grownups love it. You can substitute quinoa, orzo, couscous, or other grains in this soup, adjusting the cooking time accordingly.

1 tablespoon canola or other vegetable oil

1 small carrot, finely diced (¼ cup)

½ medium celery rib, diced (¼ cup)

1 small onion, diced (¼ cup)

1 clove garlic, finely chopped

3 cups chicken stock

½ bay leaf

½ teaspoon dried basil

3 tablespoons pearled barley

1 cup cooked turkey cut into ¾-inch cubes

3 cups loosely packed baby spinach leaves

Salt and freshly ground black pepper

1 small scallion, thinly sliced

In a medium-size saucepan, heat the oil over medium heat until hot. Stir in the carrot, celery, and onion and sauté until wilted and starting to brown, about 4 minutes. Add the garlic, cook for 30 seconds, and stir in the stock.

Add the bay leaf, basil, and barley and bring to a boil. Cover, reduce the heat so the stock is just simmering, and cook until the barley is tender, 25–30 minutes.

Remove the bay leaf. Stir in the turkey and cook until heated through. Add the spinach leaves, cook until wilted, about 2 minutes, and season to taste with salt and pepper. Stir in the scallion, ladle into bowls, and serve.

HEARTY TURKEY-VEGETABLE-BEAN SOUP

My friend Susan Kolsby shared this homey soup recipe that she makes with her favorite brother-in-law and family cooking partner, Eddy Kelly. It's filling, healthy, easy to make, and everyone enjoys it, she says. Adjust the ingredients according to what's in your refrigerator. This kind of recipe is where a salad bar or pre-cut vegetables can be helpful for buying small amounts of vegetables and beans, especially since they all go into the pan at once.

1 tablespoon extra-virgin olive oil, plus additional oil for drizzling

6 ounces ground turkey

1 medium leek, well rinsed, cut in half lengthwise, and white part thinly sliced (⅓ cup)

2 large cloves garlic, finely chopped

1½ cups chicken stock

1 cup petite diced canned tomatoes

small cauliflower florets (½ cup)

¼ pound shiitake mushrooms, stems removed and thickly sliced (½ cup)

⅓ cup baby carrots

⅓ cup canned chickpeas, rinsed and drained

¼ cup canned pinto beans, rinsed and drained

½ teaspoon dried oregano

Pinch ground cayenne pepper

Salt and freshly ground black pepper

2–3 brussels sprouts, cored and thinly sliced

2 tablespoons chopped flat-leaf parsley

In a medium-size saucepan, heat the oil over medium heat. Add the turkey and sauté until cooked through, breaking up the pieces with a wooden spatula. Stir in the leek and cook until wilted, about 3 minutes. Add the garlic and cook for 30 seconds more.

Pour in the stock and tomatoes, stirring up all browned cooking bits. Add the cauliflower, mushrooms, carrots, chickpeas, pinto beans, dried oregano, cayenne, and salt and pepper to taste. Cover and bring the soup to a gentle boil and cook until the vegetables are tender, 35–40 minutes.

Uncover, add the brussels sprouts, and cook until just tender, 4–5 minutes. Stir in the parsley, ladle the soup into bowls, drizzle on a little olive oil, and serve.

MOROCCAN TOMATO-CHICKPEA SOUP

In Morocco, harira, this fragrant and hearty soup with its warm spices, vegetables, and abundant herbs, is a popular way to break the fast during Ramadan. There are vegetarian versions (as this one is) and those with meat. Regardless of religious beliefs, it's a very pleasing soup to add to your repertoire. It was adapted from a recipe by Moroccan-born Igal Shetrit, of Riverdale, New York. I added the Harissa-Yogurt Drizzle.

1 tablespoon olive oil

1 small onion, finely chopped (¼ cup)

1 clove garlic, finely chopped

2 cups vegetable stock

½ medium celery rib, finely diced, including a few leaves if possible (¼ cup)

1 small carrot, finely diced (¼ cup)

½ medium parsnip, finely diced (¼ cup)

⅓ cup canned chickpeas, rinsed and drained

½ cup canned diced tomatoes

1½ tablespoons tomato paste

1 teaspoon ground ginger

½ teaspoon ground turmeric

¼ teaspoon ground cinnamon

2 tablespoons red lentils, washed and picked over

Salt and freshly ground black pepper

3 tablespoons finely chopped flat-leaf parsley with coarse stems removed

3 tablespoons finely chopped cilantro leaves

Harissa-Yogurt Drizzle, recipe follow (optional)

In a medium-size saucepan, heat the oil over medium heat. Stir in the onion and sauté until translucent and lightly colored, 3–4 minutes. Stir in the garlic and cook for 30 seconds. Add the stock, celery, carrots, and parsnips and bring to a boil. Cover, reduce the heat to a gentle boil, and cook until the vegetables are tender, about 10 minutes.

Stir in the chickpeas, tomatoes, tomato paste, ginger, turmeric, cinnamon, lentils, and salt and pepper to taste; simmer for 30 minutes. While the soup simmers, prepare the Harissa-Yogurt Drizzle, if using.

Before serving, stir the parsley and cilantro into the soup, ladle it into wide bowls, and garnish with a large dollop of harissa-flavored yogurt.

Harissa-Yogurt Drizzle

Harissa is a blend of sweet and savory herbs, spices, and pantry ingredients. Along with fresh herbs, frequently used spices include ginger, turmeric, saffron, cinnamon, cumin, and different peppers, including hot and sweet paprika. The condiment originally came from Tunisia, says cookbook author Paula Wolfert, but is liberally used in Morocco, as well. While in Fez, I bought harissa at a local shop in the medina that sold olives and spices. At home, I rely on the hot paste made by Dea and sold on-line and other gourmet suppliers. Harissa is also available in Middle Eastern grocery stores and some other markets.

¼ cup plain Greek yogurt

1½ teaspoons plus ¼ cup extra-virgin olive oil

½ teaspoon harissa paste

1 small clove garlic, minced

Coarse or sea salt

Stir together the yogurt, olive oil, harissa paste, garlic, and salt in a small bowl for the topping.

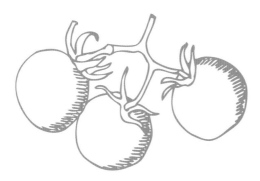

BROCCOLI-ALMOND SOUP WITH GRUYÈRE CRISPS

Although this soup tastes creamy and rich, the only cream used is the optional garnish. Toasted ground almonds and puréed broccoli thicken the soup. It's a technique dating from the Middle Ages. The soup may be made several days ahead of time, refrigerated, and returned to room temperature or heated before serving.

Shredded Gruyère baked into crunchy disks provides a nice complement to the broccoli and almond flavors. The disks may be made a couple of days ahead and kept in an airtight container.

Gruyère Crisps (recipe follows)

8 ounces broccoli florets, cut in half if large (2 cups)

2 tablespoons unsalted butter

1 large onion, thinly sliced (¾ cup)

¼ cup blanched, slivered almonds, lightly toasted (see the note)

1¾–2 cups vegetable stock

1 teaspoon ground coriander

Salt

Pinch ground white pepper

1 tablespoon sour cream (optional)

1 tablespoon light cream (optional)

Toasted Almonds

Lightly toast the almonds on a toaster oven tray at 350 degrees F. until golden, about 10 minutes, stirring occasionally. Watch that they don't burn. You could also toast them in a dry skillet over low heat.

Make the Gruyère Crisps, if serving.

In a deep, medium-size pot, steam the broccoli covered over boiling water until just tender, about 4–5 minutes once the water boils. Remove from the steamer and set aside. Reserve four small florets for garnish.

Meanwhile, in a medium-size saucepan, melt the butter over medium-low heat. Add the onion and sauté until translucent, about 4 minutes. Add the broccoli, cover, and cook over medium-low heat until the broccoli is very tender, 10–12 minutes, stirring a couple of times. Scrape the broccoli-onion mixture into the jar of an electric blender. Add the almonds, 1¾ cups of the stock, coriander, salt, and the white pepper and process until smooth.

Return the soup to the saucepan, adding the remaining stock, if needed. Taste to adjust the seasonings, and cool the soup to room temperature. Combine the sour and light creams if using, in a small bowl. Ladle the soup into heated bowls and garnish with a dollop of cream and small broccoli florets on top. Add a Gruyère Crisp and serve the remaining crisps at the table.

Gruyère Crisps

Makes about 6

1 cup coarsely shredded Gruyère or other Swiss cheese

Preheat the oven to 350 degrees F. Line a baking sheet with parchment or a silicon baking liner. Using a 2 tablespoon measure (like those used for coffee), sprinkle the cheese onto the pan in circles measuring about 3 inches in diameter. Bake until the cheese is bubbling and lightly colored, about 14 minutes. Remove from the oven and let them cool until ready to serve.

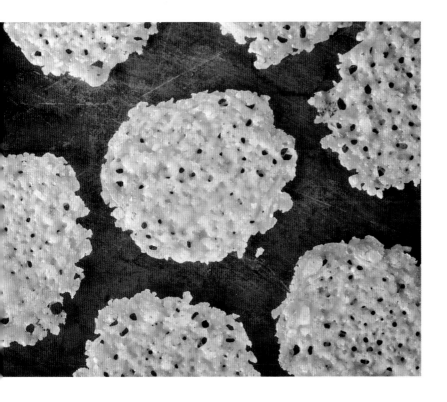

CELERY ROOT, CHESTNUT, AND GORGONZOLA SOUP

A root vegetable like celeriac combined with chestnuts makes me think of hearty foods to warm us up on chilly days. In this soup, the celery root and chestnuts are blended with robust Gorgonzola or other blue cheese and a crisp apple. The fruit's hint of sweetness elegantly balances the full flavors.

2 slices bacon, cut in half crosswise *or* 1½ tablespoons canola or other vegetable oil

¾ cup diced celery root

½ cup dry-packed, unsweetened, bottled or vacuum-sealed peeled chestnuts

1 small onion, chopped (⅓ cup)

1 medium leek, well rinsed, cut in half lengthwise, white and pale green parts thinly sliced (½ cup)

½ medium McIntosh apple, peeled, cored, and diced

1 sprig thyme

1 small bay leaf, plus 2 small sprigs for garnish

¼ teaspoon celery salt

Pinch freshly grated nutmeg

2 cups chicken stock

2 ounces crumbled Gorgonzola or other blue cheese

Salt and freshly ground white pepper

In a medium-size saucepan, cook the bacon if using, until crisp. Remove, leaving the bacon fat in the pan. Blot the bacon on paper towels, crumble it, and set aside.

Heat the bacon fat or other oil over medium heat. Add the celery root, chestnuts, onion, leek, apple, thyme, bay leaf, celery salt, and nutmeg; cover and cook until the onion and leeks are soft, about 7 minutes, stirring occasionally. Stir in the chicken stock, bring to a gentle boil, cover, and cook until the chestnuts are easily mashed, about 25 minutes. Discard the bay leaf and thyme.

Transfer the mixture to the jar of an electric blender, add the blue cheese, and purée until completely smooth. Return to the pan, season with salt and pepper, and taste to adjust the other spices, adding additional stock, if needed. The soup should have the consistency of a light cream soup and be served very hot. Ladle it into bowls, add the crumbled bacon and small sprigs of thyme on top, and serve.

Celeriac or Celery Root

This knobby, somewhat hairy, edible root may not be the prettiest vegetable in the market, but once it's thoroughly peeled, its lovely taste—milder than celery stalks—redeems it. Classically, it's used in the French salad celeriac remoulade, where it's grated and tossed with a mustard-cornichon-mayonnaise dressing. It's also used in many other stews and soups, including "Silk Purse" Roasted Leftover Root Vegetable Soup (page 95).

WEST AFRICAN PEANUT SOUP WITH CHICKEN

My good friend, cooking buddy, and neighbor Bruce Robertson told me about a peanut butter–based soup from West Africa, where he had spent a couple of years in the Peace Corps. I was intrigued. After a few tries, he liked this version. It's absolutely incomplete without the final addition of salted, chopped peanuts and lots of coarsely chopped coriander leaves.

1½ teaspoons canola or other vegetable oil

1 medium onion, chopped (½ cup)

1–2 large cloves garlic, finely chopped

1 tablespoon minced fresh ginger root

1 teaspoon ground coriander

Generous pinch cayenne pepper

1¾ cups chicken stock

¼ cup diced canned tomatoes, drained

2 tablespoons peanut butter, preferably all natural

¾ cup yam cut into 1-inch pieces

½ pound boneless, skinless chicken thighs, well trimmed and cut into bite-size pieces

Salt and freshly ground black pepper

¼ cup roasted, salted peanuts, chopped

¼ cup loosely packed cilantro leaves, coarsely chopped or torn

In a medium-size saucepan, heat the oil over medium heat. Add the onion and sauté until wilted, about 3 minutes, stirring once or twice. Stir in the garlic, ginger, coriander, and cayenne and cook for 30 seconds. Pour in 1 cup of the stock and stir up any browned bits.

Stir in the tomatoes and peanut butter and bring to a boil; reduce the heat to a slow boil. Add the yam, cover, and cook for 7 minutes. Stir in the chicken, recover, and continue cooking until the chicken and yams are cooked through, 12–15 minutes. Season to taste with salt and pepper.

Stir in the chopped peanuts and cilantro, reserving some to garnish the bowl. Ladle into two large bowls, add the remaining peanuts and cilantro, and serve.

RADISH GREENS SOUP WITH
TOASTED HAZELNUTS

Too often when buying a bunch of beets or radishes, we throw out the leafy tops. What a waste. They make a tasty, down-to-earth soup, perfect for a cold day. My good friend Pam Harding, a remarkably resourceful and talented cook, suggested this recipe. The radish version is bright green and tastes similar to sorrel. I added toasted hazelnuts and drizzled on hazelnut oil to dress it up a bit at the end. If you made the Roasted Beet Soup on page 48 and saved the greens, this soup is almost without cost.

1 tablespoon unsalted butter

1½ medium onions, diced (1 cup)

1 medium red potato, peeled and diced (¾ cup)

2 tablespoons dry white wine

2¼ cups vegetable or chicken stock

Tops from 1 bunch radishes or beets, coarse stems removed, roughly chopped (about 2 cups slightly pressed down)

2 fresh sage leaves

¼ cup milk or light cream

½ tablespoon grated lemon zest

Salt and freshly ground black pepper

2–3 teaspoons freshly squeezed lemon juice (optional)

Plain Greek yogurt for garnish

¼ cup coarsely chopped hazelnuts, toasted, for garnish

2–3 teaspoons hazelnut oil for garnish

In a medium-size saucepan, heat the butter over medium heat. Add the onion and sauté until wilted and lightly colored, 3–4 minutes. Add the potato, turning to coat with the butter. Cover and sweat over low heat until lightly colored, about 4 minutes.

Uncover, pour in the wine and stock, and stir up any browned bits. Add the greens and sage, recover, and cook until the greens are very tender, about 20 minutes.

Transfer the mixture to the jar of an electric blender and purée until smooth. Return to the pan, stir in the milk or cream, the lemon zest, season to taste with salt and pepper, and simmer until heated through.

Add lemon juice to taste if desired. Ladle the soup into bowls, garnish with a dollop of yogurt, some hazelnuts, and a drizzle of hazelnut oil around the outside edge, and serve.

SEAFOOD

Scallop and Kale Soup | 142

Spanish Lobster and Sea Scallop Chowder | 143

Clam, Potato, and Kale Soup with Bacon | 144

Provençal Mussel Soup | 147

Thai Coconut-Mussel Soup | 148

Creamy Oyster Soup with Lemon-Parsley Pesto | 150

Salmon and Corn Chowder | 153

Shrimp Posole | 154

Thai Mango-Shrimp Soup | 157

Seafood Chowder | 158

Chinese Noodle Soup with Shrimp | 161

SCALLOP AND KALE SOUP

This beautiful soup evolved while I was writing about Nova Scotia. There I met Jason Lynch, the highly regarded chef at Le Caveau restaurant at Domaine de Grand Pré Winery Restaurant, in the Annapolis Valley. After discussing the extraordinarily succulent, sweet scallops from the province's northern coastline, I asked him for a scallop soup recipe; he kindly agreed.

½ pound curly kale, center ribs removed

Coarse salt

1 tablespoon unsalted butter

1 shallot, finely chopped

1 clove garlic, finely diced

1¾ cups high-quality fish fumet or chicken stock

¼ cup heavy cream

4 large sea scallops, preferably day boat, side muscle removed

Sea salt and white pepper

1 tablespoon olive oil

Rinse the kale in cold water. Bring a medium-size pot of salted water to a boil over high heat. Add the kale and cook for 2 minutes, drain, and shock under cold water to set the color, and drain again. Transfer to a food processor and purée until smooth.

In a medium-size saucepan, melt the butter over medium-low heat. Add the shallot and garlic and sauté until they are translucent, 1–2 minutes. Stir in the stock and cream and bring to a boil over high heat. Adjust the heat down to medium and reduce the liquid to slightly more than 1½ cups, about 15 minutes.

Pat the scallops dry on a paper towel and cut in half horizontally so you end up with 8 pieces of scallop; season with salt and white pepper. In a large skillet, heat the oil over medium-high heat until hot. Add the scallops and sauté for 30 seconds per side, or until golden brown. Transfer to a plate on the side.

Stir the puréed kale into the soup base and season to taste with salt and white pepper. Ladle the soup into two bowls, add four pieces of scallop in the center of each bowl, and serve.

SPANISH LOBSTER AND SEA SCALLOP CHOWDER

In this tempting chowder, chef Jason Lynch, of Nova Scotia, celebrates the glories of this Canadian province's seafood. Lobsters and sea scallops are given a Spanish touch with smoked paprika, or Pimentón de la Vera, and slivered almonds.

1 cup loosely packed pieces of fresh potato bread or any good sourdough

¼ cup heavy cream

1½ cups water

¾ cup chicken stock

1 cloves garlic, finely chopped

2 tablespoons ground almonds (see the sidebar)

Salt and white pepper

4 medium-size scallops, side muscle removed, cut in half horizontally

1 (8-ounce) lobster tail, cooked and roughly chopped (about ¾ cup of meat)

Pinch smoked paprika for garnish

1 tablespoon slivered almonds, toasted, for garnish

1 scallion, thinly sliced on the bias, for garnish

In a bowl, soak the bread in the cream until it's absorbed, about 20 minutes. Meanwhile, in a medium-size saucepan, bring the water and stock to a boil; turn the heat down to a simmer.

In the jar of an electric blender, combine the bread and water-stock mixture, and purée until smooth. Return the soup to the saucepan, stir in the garlic and ground almonds, and season to taste with salt and white pepper. Add the scallops to the soup and simmer for 2 minutes.

Spoon the cooked lobster into the bottom of two shallow soup bowls and ladle on the hot chowder. Garnish with the smoked paprika, slivered almonds, and green scallion, and serve.

Ground Almonds

You can finely grind the almonds in either a clean coffee grinder or a food processor.

CLAM, POTATO, AND KALE SOUP
WITH BACON

In this easy seafood soup, succulent clams—in or out of their shells—with diced potatoes and kale are simmered in a fragrant broth accented with garlic, bacon, and red pepper flakes. The bacon adds a lusty flavor of its own. The soup is a variation of Portuguese caldo verde, a longtime favorite of mine. Serve it with crusty bread to sop up the broth.

2 slices bacon, chopped

1 tablespoon fragrant extra-virgin olive oil

1 medium onion, chopped (½ cup)

2 large cloves garlic, finely chopped

1½ cups chicken stock

1 medium-small Yukon Gold or other waxy potato, peeled and cut into ½-inch cubes (¾ cup)

2 small sprigs flat-leaf parsley, plus a little chopped parsley for garnish

1 small sprig thyme

Pinch red pepper flakes

12 littleneck clams, scrubbed to remove the sand

1½ cups kale leaves, preferably Lacinato variety, thick stems removed, thinly julienned crosswise (see the sidebar)

Freshly ground black pepper

In a medium-size saucepan, cook the bacon in the olive oil over medium heat until the bacon has rendered about half of its fat, 2–3 minutes. Stir in the onion and continue cooking until the onion is soft, about 5 minutes, stirring occasionally. Add the garlic and cook for 30 seconds.

Pour in the stock, stirring up any browned bits. Add the potatoes, parsley, thyme, and red pepper flakes; cover the pan, and simmer for 10 minutes. Add the clams, recover, and simmer until the clams are all opened, 8–10 minutes.

If desired, use a slotted spoon to transfer the clams to a bowl and remove them from the shells, leaving four clams in their shells for garnish. Return the liquid to a boil. Stir in the kale and cook until tender. Return the clams to the soup, season the soup to taste with pepper, and serve each bowl with a little parsley sprinkled on top.

Lacinato Kale

Kale has been used in cooking for at least two thousand years. Among the numerous varieties of edible kale (some are used only for ornamental purposes), the most common are sweet and mild curly kale (used by Jason Lynch in his recipe on page 114, because he prefers the milder flavor) and lacinato (also called Tuscan, black, or dinosaur) kale, with long, wrinkled leaves. The two are interchangeable and are usually reasonably priced. I prefer lacinato, because I find it easier to remove the stems and thick ribs by tracing along the ribs with a sharp knife.

PROVENÇAL MUSSEL SOUP

Along with mussels and diced tomatoes, this aromatic soup includes fennel, leeks, garlic, saffron, white wine, and a dash of Pernod. It's finished with a piquant mixture of minced lemon zest, parsley, and garlic that will transport you to the south of France. Enjoy the mussels in or out of their shells. (Or just add one or two of the cooked mussels in their shells to each bowl as a garnish.) Serve with toasted country bread. For a larger serving, add another half pound of mussels.

1 tablespoon fruity extra-virgin olive oil

½ fennel bulb, thinly sliced (½ cup)

1 medium leek, well rinsed, cut in half lengthwise, white and pale green parts thinly sliced (½ cup)

1 large clove garlic, minced, plus 1 additional large clove chopped for topping

1 cup bottled clam broth

1 cup dry white wine

½ cup canned diced tomatoes, preferably fire-roasted

1½ tablespoons Pernod

1 teaspoon fresh thyme leaves

¼ teaspoon saffron threads

⅛ teaspoon ground cayenne pepper

Salt

1 pound mussels, scrubbed and debearded

3 tablespoons chopped flat-leaf parsley

Zest of ½ lemon

In a medium-size saucepan, heat the oil over medium heat. Add the fennel and leek and sauté until wilted and beginning to color, about 4 minutes, stirring occasionally. Add the garlic and cook for 30 seconds. Stir in in the clam broth, wine, tomatoes, Pernod, thyme, saffron, cayenne, and salt to taste. Add the mussels, cover, and cook over medium-high heat just until the mussels open, 3–5 minutes, depending on the size.

Meanwhile, combine the parsley, lemon zest, and remaining garlic; finely chop and season with a little salt.

If desired, remove all but four of the mussels from their shells and add them back to the soup. Gently reheat the soup, stir in the topping, and taste to correct the seasonings. Ladle the soup into two wide bowls, add the reserved mussels in their shells, and serve.

THAI COCONUT-MUSSEL SOUP

This soup was inspired by a bowl of mussels I ate in Helsinki, in which lemongrass, coconut milk, and a Thai chile imparted a tantalizing Asian flavor to the broth. Serve the soup with a crisp green salad and crusty French bread to soak up every last drop of the delicious broth. Use another half pound of mussels for a more substantial meal.

1 tablespoon unsalted butter

½ medium red onion, thinly sliced

1 stalk lemongrass, trimmed and center portion minced (see the sidebar)

1 clove garlic, finely chopped

½ Thai chile *or* 1 small jalapeño pepper, seeded and very thinly sliced lengthwise

1 pound mussels, scrubbed and debearded

1½ cups chicken stock

1 (14½-ounce) can coconut milk, not "lite" variety

3 large sprigs flat-leaf parsley

Juice of ½ lemon

Salt and freshly ground black pepper

1 tablespoon julienned fresh basil

In a medium-size pot, melt the butter over medium heat. Add the onion and sauté until just wilted, about 3 minutes, stirring occasionally. Stir in the lemongrass, garlic, and chile and cook for 30 seconds.

Add the mussels, stock, coconut milk, and parsley. Cover and cook over medium-high heat just until the mussels open, 3–5 minutes, depending on size. If desired, use a slotted spoon to remove the mussels from the soup and take them out of their shells, keeping a few in their shells for garnish. Discard any mussels that are unopened or have broken shells.

Squeeze the lemon juice into the broth and season to taste with salt and pepper. Ladle the soup into two wide bowls, add the reserved mussels in their shells, sprinkle on the basil, and serve.

Using Fresh Lemongrass

There are different ways of preparing fresh lemongrass for cooking. Always start by slicing off the bottom of the bulb, removing the tough outer leaves, and trimming the stalk above the yellow section.

In some dishes, the whole stalk is bruised by hitting it with the side of a knife to release its flavor. In others, the stalk is cut in half lengthwise and then into 2- or 3-inch lengths and the pieces are bruised. That is how it is used in Thai Chicken and Coconut Milk Soup (page 185).

Finally, as in this recipe, the trimmed stalk is cut crosswise into thin slices that are either minced by hand or put into a food processor and pulverized.

I don't recommend using dried lemongrass. Rather than imparting lemongrass's fresh, citrusy flavor, I think it adds a musty, old taste.

CREAMY OYSTER SOUP WITH
LEMON-PARSLEY PESTO

Several years ago, while I was living in Washington, D.C., a friend brought me a pint of shucked oysters from a festival in St. Mary's, Maryland. She challenged me to create something "delicious." This soup of gently poached, plump oysters garnished with parsley-lemon pesto was the result. It's substantial enough for a light supper or to start an elegant dinner.

Lemon-Parsley Pesto (recipe follows)

1 tablespoon unsalted butter

1 small carrot, finely chopped (⅓ cup)

½ medium-large celery rib, finely chopped (⅓ cup)

1 small onion, finely chopped (⅓ cup)

1 clove garlic, minced

¼ cup dry vermouth

½–¾ cup half-and-half

¾ cup bottled clam broth

8 ounces shucked oysters, coarsely chopped if large, plus their liquor

Salt and white pepper

Prepare the Lemon-Parsley Pesto.

In a medium-size saucepan, melt the butter over medium heat. Stir in the carrot, celery, and onion and sauté until the onion is lightly browned, about 4 minutes, stirring occasionally. Add the garlic, cover, adjust the heat to low, and sweat the vegetables until soft, about 5 minutes.

Pour in the vermouth, stir up any browned cooking bits, and bring the liquid to a boil for 1 minute. Stir in ½ cup of the half-and-half and simmer for 5 minutes. Transfer the mixture along with the clam broth to the jar of an electric blender and purée until smooth.

Return the purée to the pan and bring it to a simmer. Add the oysters and their liquor and poach until barely done, 5–7 minutes. Season to taste with salt and white pepper. Add the remaining half-and-half if the soup is too thick. Ladle the soup into two bowls and serve with a generous tablespoon of Lemon-Parsley Pesto in the center of each.

Lemon-Parsley Pesto

1 cup loosely packed flat-leaf parsley leaves, chopped

1 large clove garlic, roughly chopped

1½ tablespoons extra-virgin olive oil

1 tablespoon unsalted butter, at room temperature

¼ teaspoon kosher or coarse sea salt

¼ cup freshly grated Parmigiano-Reggiano

Finely grated zest of ½ lemon

½–1 teaspoon freshly squeezed lemon juice

In the jar of a food processor, combine the parsley with the garlic, olive oil, butter, and salt; pulse until almost smooth and scrape into a bowl. Stir in the Parmesan cheese, lemon zest, and lemon juice to taste. Set aside.

SALMON AND CORN CHOWDER

This chowder is so satisfying, few people will guess it's also quick and easy to make, especially if you have leftover cooked salmon and corn. If not, it takes about 9 minutes to cook a slice of salmon, and frozen corn kernels work very well. Many take-out departments also sell cooked salmon.

1½ cups defrosted or fresh corn kernels, cooked

½ cup light cream or half-and-half

1 tablespoon unsalted butter

1 medium onion, chopped (½ cup)

1 cup bottled clam broth or fish stock

1 teaspoon sugar

⅓ cup poblano chile, seeds and membranes removed, chopped

½ jalapeño pepper, seeds and membranes removed, finely chopped (optional)

2 tablespoons chopped dill leaves, plus a little to add before serving

4 ounces cooked salmon, broken into small pieces

Salt and freshly ground black pepper

In a food processor, purée 1 cup of the corn with the light cream until smooth. Set aside.

In a medium-size saucepan, melt the butter over medium heat. Add the onion and sauté until wilted, 3–4 minutes. Stir in the puréed corn-cream mixture, the clam broth or fish stock, and the sugar; simmer for 2–3 minutes.

Stir in the remaining corn, poblano chile, jalapeño if using, and dill. Bring to a gentle simmer, add the salmon, and cook until the fish is heated through, 2–3 minutes. Season to taste with salt and pepper. Ladle the chowder into heated bowls, sprinkle on the remaining dill, and serve.

SHRIMP POSOLE

Native Americans have given us many culinary gifts, including clambakes from tribes in New England and this soupy stew, known as posole (or pozole), from the tribes who roamed the Southwest before Christopher Columbus arrived in the New World. It uses hominy made with dried corn kernels with the hulls and germ removed.

My friend Pam Harding introduced me to this version using shrimp. My neighbor Mark Melton, who studied Spanish for a year in Cuernavaca, said the soup is typically made with oxtail or pork in that region. He says the garnishes—thinly sliced white cabbage, radishes, and the optional avocado—elevate the soup to make it his favorite dish.

2 medium tomatillos, husked and rinsed

1 canned chipotle chile en adobo

1 tablespoons olive oil

1 medium onion, finely chopped (½ cup)

2 cloves garlic, finely chopped

½ teaspoon ground coriander

½ teaspoon ground cumin

2 cups chicken stock

1 (14-ounce) can hominy, preferably white, rinsed and drained

½ cup fresh, defrosted, or canned corn kernels

½ teaspoon dried oregano, preferably Mexican

Salt and freshly ground black pepper

6 ounces peeled and deveined large shrimp

2 tablespoons chopped fresh cilantro leaves, plus 1 tablespoon for garnish

1 tablespoon each: thinly sliced radishes and cabbage, for garnish

Diced avocado for garnish (optional)

1 lime, quartered

Bring a small pot of water to a boil; add the tomatillos, boil gently until soft, about 8 minutes, and drain. In the jar of an electric blender, combine the tomatillos and chipotle and purée until smooth.

Meanwhile, in a medium-size saucepan, heat the oil over medium heat. Add the onion and garlic, and sauté until the onion is soft, 3–4 minutes. Sprinkle on the coriander and cumin and stir until fragrant, about 1 minute. Add the tomatillo-chipotle mixture, stock, hominy, corn, and oregano; cover and simmer for 30 minutes. Remove the lid, season with salt and plenty of freshly ground black pepper, and cook for 10 minutes longer.

Add the shrimp, cover, and cook until done, 3–4 minutes. Stir in the cilantro and serve in shallow soup bowls. Add the radishes, cabbage, remaining cilantro leaves, and diced avocado if using. Squeeze on fresh lime juice to taste, and serve.

THAI MANGO-SHRIMP SOUP

Combine fresh mango and coconut milk with Thai red curry paste, ginger, and lemon grass; purée it into a smooth soup with shrimp and fresh mango salsa; and you're in for a luxurious soup with a haunting, hot-sweet taste. (See the sidebar for how to cut up a mango.)

When buying Thai curry paste, like many ethnic ingredients, I opt for brands imported from the appropriate country. Domestic brands tend to be milder, or the flavors are altered for an American audience. Adjust the amount of curry paste in this recipe to your tolerance for heat.

1 large mango, peeled and chopped (about 1 ¼ cups; ¼ cup reserved for salsa)

1 cup mango nectar, preferably aseptically packaged

1 cup canned coconut milk, not "lite" variety

½ teaspoon Thai red curry paste, or to taste

1 tablespoon finely chopped fresh lemongrass (see the sidebar "Using Fresh Lemongrass" on page 148)

1 inch fresh ginger root, peeled and coarsely chopped

1 tablespoon light brown sugar

1 tablespoon unsalted butter

10–12 large shrimp, peeled and cut into ½-inch pieces

Salt and freshly ground black pepper

2 tablespoons dark rum

For the salsa:

¼ cup mango

¼ cup finely diced red bell pepper

1 tablespoon finely julienned basil

½ tablespoon freshly squeezed lime juice

In the jar of an electric blender, combine ¾ cup mango, the mango nectar, coconut milk, curry paste, lemongrass, ginger root, and brown sugar; purée until completely smooth. Pour the soup through a strainer into a bowl, pressing to extract as much liquid as possible.

In a skillet, heat the butter over medium-high heat. Add the shrimp and sauté until just pink and cooked through, 2–3 minutes, turning frequently. Season to taste with salt and pepper. Pour in the rum and cook over high heat for 30 seconds. Scrape into the soup.

Cut the remaining ¼ cup of mango into fine cubes. In a small bowl, combine it with the red pepper, basil, and lime juice. Ladle the soup into bowls, top each with the salsa, and serve.

Peeling and Cutting Up a Mango

Start by buying a mango with a little give in it, to be sure it's ripe. Figure out which is the flat side of the mango; it corresponds with the wide side of the large seed inside. Stand the mango on one end. With a sharp paring knife, cut off one flat side as close to the seed as possible, making a large "cheek." Turn and cut off the other side along the seed. Pare away the remaining flesh around the edges in crescent shapes. Make crisscross cuts in the flesh, turn the skin inside out, and cut across the mango to slice it into nice cubes. Alternatively, once the mango cheeks are removed from the seed, you can scoop out the flesh with a large spoon and cut it into small cubes afterward.

SEAFOOD CHOWDER

What a great way to celebrate the bounty of the sea: succulent mussels, sweet scallops, shrimp, and cod (or monkfish) poached in a fragrant, creamy broth. Of course, you can change the ingredients—use clams for mussels, lobster for shrimp, and the amount of cream to your taste. This chowder is rich but not heavy. You could also use all light cream or all milk. Savor the best and freshest seafood available.

1 tablespoon unsalted butter

1 small onion, finely chopped (⅓ cup)

1 small carrot, finely chopped (¼ cup)

½ medium celery rib, finely chopped (¼ cup)

1 sprig thyme

½ bay leaf

Salt and freshly ground black pepper

¼ cup medium dry white wine

¾ cup bottled clam broth

½ cup whole milk

¼ cup heavy cream

1 medium-small Yukon Gold potato cut in ½-inch cubes (¾ cup)

8 mussels, scrubbed and debearded

4 ounces cod or monkfish fillet, cut into 1-inch pieces

4 ounces bay or quartered sea scallops

6–8 large shrimp, peeled and deveined

Pinch cayenne pepper

2 tablespoons chopped flat-leaf parsley

In a deep, medium-size pan, heat the butter over medium heat. Stir in the onion, carrot, celery, thyme, and bay leaf; cover and sweat over medium-low heat until the vegetables are tender, 8–10 minutes. Season to taste with salt and freshly ground black pepper.

Pour in the wine and boil for a minute; stir in the clam broth, milk, and cream. Add the potatoes and simmer until they are almost tender when pierced with the tip of a knife, about 8 minutes.

Add the mussels, cod or monkfish, scallops, and shrimp. Simmer until all the shells are open and the fish and shellfish are just cooked through, 5–7 minutes. Remove the thyme and bay leaf, taste to adjust the seasoning, add the cayenne if desired. Discard any mussels that have not opened. Ladle into bowls, sprinkle on the parsley, and serve.

CHINESE NOODLE SOUP WITH SHRIMP

This is my version of Chinese noodle soup with snow peas, carrots, and mushrooms accompanied by noodles. Since it isn't really classic, you could add whatever you like and make the broth as spicy as you like. Sometimes I add six ounces of peeled and deveined large shrimp along with the snow peas to the broth as it simmers. Add hot chile sauce if you like spicy soup. Fresh Chinese-style noodles are available in the refrigerated section of supermarkets, or use dried noodles.

½ cup cooked Chinese-style noodles (2 ounces)

1½ teaspoons canola or other vegetable oil

½ cup stemmed and thickly sliced shiitake or cremini mushrooms

3 (⅛-inch-thick) slices peeled ginger root, cut into thin matchsticks (about 1 tablespoon)

1 clove garlic, thinly sliced

1½ cups vegetable stock

1 tablespoon hoisin sauce

2 teaspoons soy sauce

½ cup sliced scallions, including white and light green parts (2 scallions), a few slices reserved for garnish

1 small carrot, sliced (¼ cup)

¼ cup sliced canned water chestnuts

⅓ cup snow peas, strings removed, cut on the bias into thirds

2 teaspoons spicy or plain sesame oil

1–2 tablespoons freshly squeezed lime juice

3 tablespoons chopped cilantro leaves

Hot chile sauce, to taste (optional)

In a small saucepan, cook the noodles in boiling water until just tender, about 3 minutes if already soft, or longer if dried. Drain and set aside.

In a medium-size saucepan, heat the oil over medium heat until hot. Stir in the mushrooms and ginger and cook until the mushrooms are wilted, about 3 minutes, stirring frequently. Stir in the garlic, cook for 30 seconds; then pour in the stock, stirring up any browned cooking bits. Add the hoisin sauce and soy sauce and bring to a simmer.

Add the scallions, carrots, and water chestnuts, cook for 3 minutes, then add the snow peas and simmer about 2 minutes. Stir in the reserved noodles, add the sesame oil and lime juice to taste. Stir about half of the cilantro into the soup. Add hot chile sauce to taste, ladle the soup into bowls, and serve with the remaining cilantro and scallion slices sprinkled on top.

POULTRY

Greek Lemon Chicken and Rice Soup | 165

Far-Better-Than-Canned Chicken Noodle Soup | 166

Chicken Soup for the Soul | 168

Chicken-Vegetable and Orzo Soup | 171

Japanese Chicken and Noodle Soup | 172

Malaysian Chicken Laksa | 175

Jamaican Jerk Chicken Soup with Coconut, Plantains, and Peppers | 176

Mexican Chicken Tortilla Soup | 179

Scottish Cock-a-Leekie Soup | 180

Thai Chicken and Coconut Milk Soup | 185

Circassian Chicken Soup | 186

Leftover Turkey and Tomatillo Soup | 188

Gascon Duck Confit and Vegetable Soup | 190

GREEK LEMON CHICKEN AND RICE SOUP

This thick, lemony chicken soup with rice, or avgolemono, is a Greek classic that takes a minimum of effort. It's a perfect rainy day lunch or even light supper. My version is slightly more rustic and colorful than some because I leave the minced carrot, onion, and celery in the stock rather than straining them out. Be sure to use fresh lemon juice. It makes a big difference. As with all egg-thickened sauces and soups, it's important not to let the soup boil, or the eggs will curdle.

1½ teaspoons olive or vegetable oil

1 small carrot, finely chopped (¼ cup)

½ medium celery rib, finely chopped (¼ cup)

1 very small or half a medium onion, finely chopped (¼ cup)

7–8 ounces boneless, skinless chicken thighs or breasts, cut into ½ inch cubes

2 cups chicken stock

1 tablespoon chopped flat-leaf parsley

2 tablespoons uncooked white rice

1 large egg

2 tablespoons freshly squeezed lemon juice, or more to taste

Salt and freshly ground black pepper

In a medium-size saucepan, heat the oil over medium-high heat until hot. Stir in the carrot, celery, and onion and sauté until the vegetables are softened, about 5 minutes.

Add the chicken, stock, and parsley and bring the liquid to a boil. Stir in the rice, cover, and reduce the heat so the liquid is barely simmering. Cook until the rice is tender, about 20 minutes.

In a small bowl, beat the egg and lemon juice together until smooth. Slowly whisk about ¾ cup of the hot stock into the egg-lemon mixture, beating constantly. Stir the warmed egg mixture into the soup. Season to taste with salt and pepper. Add a few more drops of lemon juice if desired. Heat gently, but do not let the liquid boil. Serve at once or keep warm over low heat until ready to serve.

FAR-BETTER-THAN-CANNED
CHICKEN NOODLE SOUP

If you crave a bowl of consoling chicken noodle soup, this one is easy to make, and, as the title claims, is far better than commercial alternatives. You can make it with leftover cooked chicken. While I think dark meat stays juicier and has more flavor, many people prefer white meat, but the choice is yours. Even if you use cooked meat, a couple of added wings will enrich the stock. Add the noodles shortly before you serve the soup.

1½ teaspoons canola or other vegetable oil

½ medium celery rib, diced (¼ cup)

1 very small or half a medium onion, diced (¼ cup)

3 cups chicken stock, bolstered with 2 chicken wings, if desired

1 medium carrot, sliced (½ cup)

¼ teaspoon dried basil

¼ teaspoon dried oregano

1 cup diced cooked chicken thigh or breast meat

¾ cup cooked egg noodles

1 tablespoon chopped flat-leaf parsley

Salt and freshly ground black pepper

In a medium-size saucepan, heat the oil over medium heat. Stir in the celery and onion and sauté until tender, about 5 minutes. Add the stock, chicken wings if using, carrots, basil, and oregano and bring the liquid to a boil. Reduce the heat, cover, and simmer for 20 minutes.

Uncover, add the cooked chicken meat and noodles, and simmer until heated through, 5–7 minutes. Stir in the parsley, season with salt and pepper to taste, ladle into bowls, and serve.

Note: As an alternative, use 2 chicken thighs on the bone, with or without skin, and add them at the beginning with the stock. Once cooked, remove the thighs, cut the meat into pieces, and return the meat to the soup. Discard the bones. This replaces the diced chicken in the recipe.

Economize by Buying the Whole Chicken

Whole chickens are reasonably priced. With a little planning, one medium-size chicken (about 3½ pounds) can become a part of several soups. It's important, however, that all the pieces are either cooked or frozen within two days of bringing the bird home.

Start by cutting off the wings and freezing them in a resealable plastic bag for a rainy day or any time you want Far-Better-Than-Canned Chicken Noodle Soup. Remove the skin, chop it into pieces, put it into a plastic bag, and refrigerate or freeze until you have time to slowly cook the pieces in a large skillet over low heat into "cracklings." With a little salt added, these make the best crunchy topping ever.

Use one boned, uncooked breast cutlet for Thai Chicken and Coconut Milk Soup or Greek Lemon Chicken and Rice Soup. Cook the other breast on or off the bone, wrap it well, and keep it in the refrigerator for up to three to four days. It can be diced and added to Mexican Chicken Tortilla Soup or finely chopped for the meatballs in Circassian Chicken Soup. The meat can also be added to any other noodle or vegetable soups to turn them into a main course.

The two thighs are about what's needed for Malaysian Chicken Laksa, West African Peanut Soup with Chicken, and several other soups in this book. The legs may also be used in those soups. Alternatively, you could season them with salt, pepper, and some spices of your choice, sauté them in a skillet, and enjoy them alongside a soup.

Finally, freeze any uncooked bones and trimmings to enrich future soups.

CHICKEN SOUP FOR THE SOUL

Grandmothers, great grandmothers, and countless celebrated chefs throughout the ages have simmered capons, fowl, and other large chickens into a golden-colored nectar for the soul and as an antidote for the common cold and a raft of other maladies. I adapted Carole Walter's family-size recipe, so two can enjoy this treat. Add noodles if you like. Carole points out that there is natural salt in many ingredients, so taste before adding additional salt.

Matzo Balls (recipe follows; optional)

2 chicken wings (see "Economize by Buying the Whole Chicken" on page 167)

1 medium carrot, cut into 3-inch pieces

1 medium celery rib (½ cup), including leaves if possible, cut into 3-inch pieces

½ cup medium onion, stuck with 2 cloves

1-inch piece of dark greens from 1 leek, rinsed (optional)

4 cups low-sodium chicken stock

1 small bay leaf

2 sprigs flat-leaf parsley, plus 1 tablespoon chopped leaves, to add at the end

Salt, if needed, and freshly ground black pepper

1 tablespoon chopped fresh dill leaves

If serving matzo balls, make them the night before.

In a medium-size pot, combine the chicken wings, carrot, celery, onion, leek if using, and 3 cups of the stock and bring to a boil over high heat. Add the bay leaf and parsley sprigs; reduce the heat, cover, and simmer for 40 minutes. Remove the wings and carrots and set aside. Discard the bay leaf.

Strain the remaining soup into a clean pot, pressing to extract as much liquid as possible. Taste and add more stock—or water if the soup is salty. Cut about half of the carrot pieces, or more if you like carrots, into slices and reserve. (Eat or discard any extras.) Remove the meat from the wings (there won't be a lot) and tear it into shreds. Return the reserved carrots and chicken to the soup. Heat the soup until hot, season with salt, if needed, and pepper. Add the matzo balls and simmer until heated through. Stir in the remaining parsley and the dill and serve.

Matzo Balls

When you want a perfect matzo ball, ask someone like Carole Walter, a beloved Jewish mother and grandmother. This is her recipe, and because it makes just 5–6 matzo balls, you don't have to wait for the holidays to enjoy it. Carole says, "No peeking please while they boil." Matzo balls swell to at least double their size when fully cooked.

1 large egg

2 tablespoons club soda, chicken broth, or water

2½ teaspoons melted chicken fat or canola oil

¼ cup matzo meal

¼ teaspoon salt

Freshly ground black pepper

½ tablespoon minced flat-leaf parsley

In a bowl, using a handheld mixer or whisk, beat the egg until light and foamy. Beat in the club soda or other liquid and chicken fat or oil.

Whisk in the matzo meal, salt, black pepper to taste, and parsley, rapidly mixing continuously until well blended. Once the ingredients are incorporated, it is important to never stir the batter again. Cover the bowl with plastic wrap and chill overnight or for at least 6–8 hours.

Bring a large pot of salted water to a boil. Have ready a bowl of ice water for moistening your hands if needed. Using a 1 teaspoon measure, scoop a rounded ball of dough about the size of a large walnut onto one of your moistened hands and roll it into a ball using both hands. As each ball is formed, drop it into the boiling water.

When all the balls are in the water, cover the pot, reduce the heat, and gently boil for 40–45 minutes. Drain well in a colander, empty into a bowl, and cover with plastic wrap until ready to use.

To serve, gently reheat the matzo balls in the hot chicken soup and serve immediately. Don't allow the matzo balls to sit too long in the soup, as they will absorb too much of the broth and turn the soup cloudy.

CHICKEN-VEGETABLE AND ORZO SOUP

When my children were young, they originally thought chicken-vegetable soup with pasta came from a red and white can. I tried to introduce healthier versions—even replacing the original with my homemade soup in the can—but they initially spurned my efforts. Thank goodness, we've all moved forward. Even though the ingredients in this soup are pretty basic, I find it quite soothing and satisfying. With leftover chicken in the refrigerator, it's a snap. If the soup sits for several hours or is reheated, you may need to add more stock.

1 tablespoon canola or other vegetable oil

1 small carrot, diced (¼ cup)

½ medium celery rib, diced (¼ cup)

1 small or half medium onion, diced (¼ cup)

1 large clove garlic, minced

2 cups chicken stock

½ teaspoon dried thyme leaves

½ bay leaf

2 tablespoons dried alphabet pasta or orzo

⅓ cup frozen corn

⅓ cup frozen petite peas

1 cup diced cooked chicken, light or dark meat

2 tablespoons chopped flat-leaf parsley

Salt and freshly ground black pepper

In a medium-size saucepan, heat the oil over medium-high heat until hot. Stir in the carrots, celery, and onion and sauté until lightly browned, 4–5 minutes, stirring often so they don't burn. Add the garlic and cook for 30 seconds. Pour in the stock and stir up any browned cooking bits. Add the thyme and bay leaf and simmer for 15 minutes.

Meanwhile, cook the dried pasta in salted boiling water according to the package directions. Drain and set aside.

Stir the corn and peas into the soup and simmer for 7 minutes. Add the chicken and continue to cook until heated through. Remove the bay leaf, stir in the drained pasta and the parsley, season to taste with salt and pepper, ladle into bowls, and serve.

JAPANESE CHICKEN AND NOODLE SOUP

While living in San Francisco, I discovered tori no mizutaki, a Japanese one-dish chicken in a pot, in a now-shuttered restaurant on Union Street. Chicken, shiitakes, and vegetables are simmered in a dashi broth and served with ponzu sauce for dipping. Some versions include diced tofu and cellophane noodles, as well.

Dashi stock or soup base can be found in Japanese groceries and on the Internet. Some have MSG, which I avoid, so I make a simple broth with dried seaweed or kelp (dashi) and water. Traditionally, when several people dine together, they share the same pot of soup. For two, ladle the ingredients into wide bowls and serve a small dish of dipping sauce on the side.

1 tablespoon dried seaweed flakes

1½ cups water

2 teaspoons sesame oil

1 large clove garlic, chopped

4 ounces shiitake mushrooms, wiped, coarse stems removed, and cut into ¼-inch slices

½ pound skinless, boneless chicken thighs, cut into bite-size pieces

1 baby bok choy, sliced crosswise into ¾-inch slices

3 large scallions including green parts, trimmed and sliced diagonally into 2-inch pieces (about 1 cup)

½ cup peeled and thinly sliced young carrots

½ cup soaked cellophane noodles (optional)

½ cup tofu, cut into ½-inch cubes

½ cup ponzu sauce for dipping

Pinch red pepper flakes

Toasted sesame seeds for garnish

In a small saucepan, combine the seaweed and water and bring just to a boil over medium-high heat; strain into a clean bowl, pressing to extract as much liquid as possible. You should have about 1¼ cups of liquid. Set it aside.

In a medium-size saucepan, heat 1 teaspoon of the oil over medium heat. Add the garlic and sauté for 30 seconds. Stir in the remaining teaspoon of oil and the mushrooms and cook for 1 minute, stirring often. Add the chicken and sauté until lightly colored on all sides, 3–4 minutes.

Pour in the reserved seaweed broth, add the bok choy, scallions, and carrots, and bring the liquid to a boil. Reduce the heat and simmer until the vegetables are tender, 5–6 minutes. Add the cellophane noodles and tofu if using. Stir in 3 tablespoons of the ponzu sauce and red pepper flakes and cook for 1 minute more. Ladle the soup into bowls, sprinkle on the sesame seeds, and serve hot with the remaining ponzu sauce on the side for dipping.

MALAYSIAN CHICKEN LAKSA

While traveling throughout Malaysia a few years ago, I fell in love with the complex flavors in the food. Many dishes, like this fragrant, coconut curry noodle soup, start with a fairly long list of ingredients. Once the spices are ground, however, the soup is fairly straightforward and takes about 30 minutes. Sambal oelek—a hot chile paste available in the Asian section of many supermarkets—is added to taste at the end. There are Malaysian curry spice mixtures on the Internet, but I can't attest to their quality. If you prefer, substitute white rice for the rice noodles.

1 tablespoon coriander seeds

½ teaspoon *each* black peppercorns, cumin seeds, and fennel seeds

4 whole cloves

½ teaspoon ground turmeric

1 dried árbol chile, stemmed

1 lemongrass stalk, trimmed and coarse outer leaves removed

1½ tablespoons canola or other vegetable oil

½ pound boneless, skinless chicken thighs, cut into 1-inch cubes

½ teaspoon shrimp paste

¼ cup thinly sliced shallots

2–2½ cups chicken stock

¾ cup canned coconut milk, not "lite" variety

2 teaspoons palm sugar or light brown sugar

1 cinnamon stick

Salt

3 ounces wide rice noodles

Sambal oelek (optional)

3 tablespoons torn mint leaves

3 tablespoons torn cilantro leaves

1 lime, cut into wedges

In a clean coffee mill or spice grinder, grind the coriander, peppercorns, cumin, fennel, cloves, turmeric, and chile into a powder. Using a meat pounder, bruise the lemongrass along the stalk.

In a medium-size saucepan, heat the oil over medium heat. Add the spice mixture—not the lemongrass—and stir until just fragrant, 5–7 seconds. Add the chicken, shrimp paste, and shallots and stir constantly for 2 minutes to blend completely.

Pour in the 2 cups of stock and coconut milk; add the sugar, cinnamon stick, about ½ teaspoon of salt, and lemongrass. Bring the soup to a boil, then reduce the heat, cover, and simmer for 20 minutes.

Meanwhile, bring a pot of water to a boil and cook the noodles (or rice) until al dente. Drain, add to the soup, and cook for 1–2 minutes longer.

Remove and discard the cinnamon stick and lemongrass. Taste to adjust the seasonings, adding the remaining stock if the soup is too thick. Add the sambal oelek to taste if desired. Ladle the soup into bowls, sprinkle on the mint and cilantro, and serve with lime wedges.

JAMAICAN JERK CHICKEN SOUP WITH COCONUT, PLANTAINS, AND PEPPERS

This colorful chicken soup is filled with layers of tropical flavors, including jerk seasoning, coconut milk, and dark rum. There are several varieties of jerk seasoning, including powdered spice blends. I prefer Walkerswood traditional Jamaican jerk seasoning paste that is made in Jamaica. It has quite a lot of heat, but they also sell a mild version.

2 tablespoons coconut or vegetable oil

½ pound boneless, skinless chicken thighs, excess fat removed, patted dry, and cut into large cubes

1 tablespoon all-purpose flour

Salt and freshly ground black pepper

1½ teaspoons grated fresh ginger root

1½ teaspoons finely chopped garlic

1½ cups chicken stock

⅓ cup coconut milk, not "lite" variety

1½ teaspoons palm sugar or light brown sugar

2 teaspoons freshly squeezed lime juice, plus the grated zest of 1 lime

1 teaspoon soy sauce

1 teaspoon jerk seasoning paste

½ cup fresh or canned pineapple in juice, cut into small cubes

2 scallions, including green parts, sliced

¼ cup diced red pepper (about half a pepper)

¼ cup diced green bell pepper (about half a pepper)

½ ripe plantain (optional; see the sidebar)

1½ tablespoons dark rum

2 tablespoons julienned fresh basil leaves

Toasted coconut and lime wedges for garnish

In a medium-size saucepan, heat 1 tablespoon of the oil over medium-high heat until hot. Toss the chicken in the flour, add the pieces to the pan, taking care not to crowd, and quickly brown them on all sides. Remove with a slotted spoon to a bowl and season with salt and pepper.

Add another teaspoon of oil to the pan along with the ginger and garlic and any remaining flour. Cook for 1 minute; stir in the stock, coconut milk, sugar, lime juice and zest, soy sauce, and jerk seasoning paste and bring to a boil. Reduce the heat, add the pineapple, scallions, and bell peppers and simmer for 10 minutes.

Meanwhile, peel the plantain if using and cut it into ½-inch slices. Heat the remaining oil in a small skillet over medium-high heat until hot. Add the plantain slices and sauté until brown on both sides, turning once, 2–3 minutes. Remove and cut each slice in half.

Add them to the pan with the pineapple and vegetables, along with the chicken, and continue cooking until the chicken is just cooked through, 7–9 minutes. Raise the heat to high, stir in the rum and basil leaves, taste to adjust the seasonings, and serve garnished with coconut and lime wedges.

Plantains by the Color

In spite of a resemblance to bananas, plantains are generally larger and neither taste like nor have the same texture as bananas. Young plantains are green and quite starchy. As they mature, they become yellow with black spots. It's not until they are totally black that they are ripe, soft, and sweet. They are very popular in Caribbean cooking. You could substitute a slightly underripe banana.

MEXICAN CHICKEN TORTILLA SOUP

One of the most beloved soups in Mexican kitchens, this version is adapted from Ivy Stark, the executive chef of the Dos Caminos restaurants, with whom I coauthored two books. The heat of the chiles, and chicken soup's well-known nurturing goodness make this a dish to warm your mouth and your soul. Roasted tomatoes puréed with chiles and crisp tortilla chips make it hearty enough to be eaten as a main course for lunch on a cold day. Add more chicken for heartier appetites. Like most soups, this tortilla soup is better on the second day, after the flavors have blended.

3 plum tomatoes, cut in half lengthwise

2 tablespoons olive oil

Kosher salt and freshly ground black pepper

1 medium onion, coarsely chopped (½ cup)

3 cloves garlic, chopped

2 dried guajillo chiles, toasted

2 dried pasilla chiles, toasted

1 bay leaf

3 cups chicken stock, preferably homemade

¾ cup broken corn tortilla chips, plus extra for garnish

1 ripe avocado, peeled, seeded, and cut into ½-inch cubes

8 ounces boneless, skinless chicken breast, grilled and cut into ½-inch cubes

3 ounces queso fresco, cut into ½-inch cubes (see the sidebar for Mexican Meatball Soup on page 217)

3 tablespoons chopped cilantro leaves

Preheat the oven to 400 degrees F.

In an oven-safe baking dish, toss the tomatoes with 1 tablespoon of the olive oil, sprinkle with salt and pepper, and roast for about 15 minutes, or until the skin is brown and blistered. Remove and let cool.

In a large soup pot, heat the remaining tablespoon of olive oil over medium heat. Add the onion and sauté until translucent, about 5 minutes; add the garlic and cook until soft, 30 seconds–1 minute Stir in the chiles, roasted tomatoes, bay leaf, and chicken stock and simmer for 20 minutes. Remove the bay leaf, add half the tortilla chips, and purée the soup in batches in a food processor or electric blender until smooth. Season to taste with salt and pepper. Return the soup to the pot and reheat if necessary.

Ladle the soup into two wide soup bowls. Add the avocado, chicken, queso fresco, and cilantro along with a sprinkle of the remaining tortilla chips.

SCOTTISH COCK-A-LEEKIE SOUP

In early Scotland, cock-a-leekie soup was supposedly made with an old bird (a cock) simmered with leeks. Barley was added to thicken the broth. Oxford University food historians report the first printed recipe comes from the end of the sixteenth century, but the name came into use only in the eighteenth century. Some early recipes included prunes in the broth. In my modern interpretation, I use boneless chicken thighs and leeks, with a few dried cranberries to impart a tart-sweet accent.

1 tablespoon unsalted butter

2 cups white and pale green parts of leeks, well rinsed, cut in half lengthwise and thinly sliced

½ medium celery rib, thinly sliced (¼ cup)

3 cups chicken stock

2 tablespoons pearled barley

2 tablespoons chopped flat-leaf parsley, plus 2 teaspoons for garnish

1 small sprig fresh thyme *or* ¼ teaspoon dried

1 small bay leaf *or* ½ large bay leaf

½ pound boneless, skinless chicken thighs, excess fat removed (2 medium thighs)

Salt and freshly ground black pepper

¼ cup dried cranberries (optional)

2–3 tablespoons light cream

In a medium-size saucepan, melt the butter over medium-high heat. Stir in the leeks and celery and sauté until wilted and lightly colored, 3–4 minutes, stirring occasionally. Pour in the stock, stirring up any browned bits. Add the barley, parsley, thyme, and bay leaf; cover and simmer for 15 minutes.

Uncover and add the chicken, recover, and continue simmering until the barley is tender and the chicken is cooked through, about 15 minutes more. Season to taste with salt and pepper, and add the cranberries if using. Stir in the cream and simmer until hot. Remove the bay leaf and thyme sprig, ladle the soup into bowls, add the remaining parsley, and serve.

THAI CHICKEN AND COCONUT MILK SOUP

To make this classic Thai soup, Tom Kha Gai, use authentic ingredients from a Thai grocer or online purveyor. There you'll easily find lemongrass, straw mushrooms, the thin, yet very hot bird's eye chiles, fish sauce, palm sugar, kaffir lime leaves, as well as galangal all in one place. Galangal, like fresh ginger, is a rhizome. Its taste is similar to ginger but stronger. Bruising lemongrass and kaffir leaves by hitting them with a meat pounder or the side of your knife helps to release their flavor. As a main course, serve with steamed jasmine rice on the side.

2 cups low-sodium chicken stock

1 cup coconut milk, preferably fresh, but canned will work if not "lite"

1-inch piece of fresh galangal, thinly sliced crosswise

1 lemongrass stalk, trimmed and outer leaves removed, cut into 2-inch pieces, and bruised (see the sidebar "Using Fresh Lemongrass" on page 148)

3–4 fresh kaffir lime leaves, center ribs removed, bruised and torn in half

8 ounces trimmed, boneless, skinless chicken breast, cut into 1-inch pieces

4 ounces mild fresh mushrooms, such as straw, maitake, or oyster mushrooms, stemmed and quartered or cut into bite-size pieces

2–3 fresh red bird's eye chiles, according to taste, seeded if desired, and sliced into thin lengthwise strips *or* substitute 1 small serrano chile

¼ cup freshly squeezed lime juice (2 limes), plus 1 lime, quartered, to serve with the soup

¼ cup Thai (*nam pla*) or Vietnamese (*nuoc mam*) fish sauce

1 teaspoon palm sugar *or* light brown sugar

¼ cup fresh cilantro leaves, torn or coarsely chopped

Steamed jasmine rice (optional)

In a small saucepan or skillet, reduce the chicken stock over high heat to 1 cup.

In a medium-size saucepan, combine the reduced stock, coconut milk, galangal, lemongrass, and kaffir lime leaves; slowly bring to just under a simmer and cook for 5 minutes. Add the chicken and mushrooms and cook until the chicken is done, 8–10 minutes, stirring often. Do not let the soup boil. When the chicken is cooked, add the chiles, and remove the pan from the heat.

In a small bowl, combine the lime juice, fish sauce, and palm sugar; mix into the soup. Taste to adjust the flavors, adding more lime juice and fish sauce, according to taste, and more stock or water if needed. Remove the lemongrass and lime leaves. Stir in the cilantro and serve with extra wedges of lime, and with jasmine rice if you wish.

Soup Builds Friendships

I've said many times, soups create friendships. Throughout this book there are soups from friends across the United States and around the world. This recipe for Chicken and Coconut Milk came from Jessica Craig-Martin, a highly regarded photographer who was seated next to me in a Thai restaurant while I was on a lunch break from jury duty. We chatted, discovered our shared love for Thai food and cooking, in general, and Jessica sent me this recipe. We both agree that shopping in ethnic markets is an exciting—and tasty—adventure.

CIRCASSIAN CHICKEN SOUP

Like Turkish Eggplant Soup inspired by Imam Bayildi, on page 96, this soup is based on a traditional Turkish appetizer. Circassian Chicken is made with minced chicken breast in a seasoned walnut and bread sauce. I turned the combination into small meatballs poached in a flavorful broth. Serve this soup at room temperature or heated.

For the soup:

4 cups chicken stock

⅓ cup sliced carrots

⅓ cup sliced celery

1 large clove garlic, thinly sliced

1 bay leaf

2 teaspoons hot or sweet paprika

2 tablespoons chopped flat-leaf parsley for garnish

Salt and freshly ground black pepper

Cayenne pepper

1 tablespoon walnut oil and a few walnut pieces for garnish

For the meatballs:

1 extra large egg yolk

½ teaspoon ras al hanout (see the sidebar on page 95)

⅓ cup walnut pieces

½ cup finely chopped cooked chicken breast, chilled for about 15 minutes

1 small or ½ medium onion, chopped (¼ cup)

1 tablespoon minced flat-leaf parsley

Pinch salt

Freshly ground black pepper

In a medium-size saucepan, reduce the chicken stock over high heat from 4 cups to 3 cups. Add the carrots, celery, garlic, bay leaf, and paprika. Bring to a boil, reduce the heat to a simmer to keep warm.

In a small bowl, whisk together the egg yolk and ras al hanout. In a food processor, pulse ⅓ cup of walnuts until almost a powder with few little pieces. Don't let the machine run until the walnuts become a paste.

Add the chicken, onion, the tablespoon of parsley, salt and pepper, and the seasoned egg yolk; pulse until the mixture comes together. Using your hands, form the mixture into 6–8 walnut-size meatballs. Slide them into the soup and simmer until they are cooked through and rise to the surface, about 5 minutes. Using a slotted spoon, transfer them to two wide bowls.

Stir 2 tablespoons of parsley into the soup, season to taste with salt, pepper, and cayenne, and ladle the soup into the bowls. Drizzle on the walnut oil, add a few walnut pieces, and serve.

Soup Names

Ottoman sultans had an appetite for the finest of everything in their empire, and women from north of the Caucasus Mountains were famed for their fine features and beautiful light skin. They were often captured and brought to the harem in Istanbul's Topkapi Palace to serve as wives and concubines. The dish is named for the pale complexions of Circassian women.

LEFTOVER TURKEY AND TOMATILLO SOUP

I became a fan of tomatillos' tangy taste in salsas and soups after coauthoring three Mexican cookbooks. Although tomatillos resemble green tomatoes, once their papery husks are removed the flesh inside is meatier and paler in color. Dress this soup up with sour cream, sliced scallions, and Crispy Tortillas Strips. You can substitute chicken, shrimp, or even tofu for the turkey in this recipe.

3 medium tomatillos (about 10 ounces), husked, rinsed, and chopped

1 cup chicken or vegetable stock

1 tablespoon olive oil

1/3 cup diced onion

2 cloves garlic, minced

1/3 cup diced green bell pepper

1 teaspoon ground cumin

1/2 teaspoon chile powder

1/2 serrano chile, minced, with or without seeds according to taste

1/3 cup corn kernels, defrosted or fresh

1 cup cooked turkey cut into 3/4-inch cubes

Crispy Tortilla Strips (recipe follows) or taco chips

1/3 cup loosely packed chopped cilantro leaves

Salt and freshly ground black pepper

2 tablespoons sour cream or plain Greek yogurt

1 small scallion, white and pale green parts, thinly sliced

In the jar of an electric blender, combine half of the chopped tomatillos with the stock and purée until smooth. Set aside.

In a medium-size saucepan, heat the oil over medium heat. Add the onion and sauté until translucent, 3–4 minutes. Stir in the garlic and cook for 30 seconds. Add the green bell pepper, the remaining tomatillos, cumin, and chile powder; cover and sweat over low heat for 7 minutes or until the tomatillos begin to break down.

Pour the reserved puréed tomatillo-stock mixture into the pan, add the serrano chile and corn to the pan, cover, and simmer for 15 minutes or until the vegetables are all very tender, stirring occasionally. Add the turkey and cook until warmed through.

Meanwhile, make the Crispy Tortilla Strips.

Sprinkle the cilantro into the soup, stir once or twice, ladle into bowls, and add a dollop of sour cream, some sliced scallions, and the tortilla strips.

Crispy Tortilla Strips

Canola or other vegetable oil

1 corn tortilla, cut into ¼-inch-wide strips

Salt

Cayenne pepper (optional)

In a small skillet, add enough oil to measure about ¼ inch deep and heat over medium heat until a small drop of water sizzles when dropped in the pan. Add the tortilla strips and fry until golden, turning often. Pour into a strainer, then blot dry on paper towels. Season to taste with salt and, if desired, cayenne pepper, and toss again.

GASCON DUCK CONFIT AND VEGETABLE SOUP

This rustic, peasant-style duck soup meal is typical of the lusty food from Gascony. It comes from Ariane Daguin, a true Gascon. There are as many varieties of this much-loved classic as there are cooks in the region. Enjoy it on a chilly evening, served with thick slices of country bread.

A confit of duck has been slowly cooked in its own fat to preserve it. Fortunately, this delicious, but time-consuming delicacy is available in many gourmet stores or online. I love the just duck and vegetables combination. But for a more robust meal, prepare the sausage omelet and add it toward the end of the cooking.

For the soup:

2 teaspoons rendered duck fat or vegetable oil

2 large cloves garlic, chopped

¾ cup white and pale green parts of a leek, well rinsed, lengthwise and thinly sliced

½ medium celery rib, diced (¼ cup)

⅓ cup pancetta or unsmoked bacon, cut into small pieces

2 cups duck or chicken stock

1 purchased duck leg confit, cut in half, skin and bones removed, and meat torn into pieces

1 small baby bok choy, cut crosswise into ½-inch slices

1 medium carrot, sliced on the diagonal (½ cup)

4 cloves roasted garlic (see the sidebar)

For the sausage omelet:

2 large eggs

4 ounces pork sausage, casing removed, broken into small pieces

1½ tablespoons chopped flat-leaf parsley

2 teaspoons rendered duck fat or vegetable oil

Salt and freshly ground black pepper

In a medium-size saucepan, heat the duck fat or oil over medium-high heat. Stir in the garlic, leek, celery, and pancetta and sauté until tender, about 5 minutes, stirring occasionally. Pour in the stock and bring the liquid to a boil. Reduce the heat and add the duck, bok choy, carrot, and roasted garlic cloves; simmer until the vegetables are tender, 10–15 minutes.

Meanwhile, prepare the sausage omelet if serving. Begin by preheating the oven to 375 degrees F.

In a bowl, beat the eggs with the sausage and parsley. In a 10-inch nonstick skillet, heat the duck fat or vegetable oil over medium-high heat. Pour in the egg mixture, shaking the pan to distribute evenly, and cook until the first side is golden, about 3 minutes. Transfer the pan to the oven and bake until the top is set, 6–7 minutes.

Remove the pan from the oven, cut the omelet into large squares, slide them into the stock, and simmer for a few minutes. Ladle the soup into warm, large, flat bowls, dividing the duck and vegetables evenly, and serve.

Roasted Garlic

Rather than roasting a head of garlic in the oven, put whatever number of large peeled cloves you want—from four, for this recipe, to up to a cup—in a small saucepan or skillet and cover with olive oil. Cook over medium to medium-low heat until the cloves are tender and golden brown, stirring often. The time can vary widely depending on the number of cloves, but it should be somewhere around 30 minutes. If the garlic is burning without becoming tender, adjust the heat down. Remove and strain in a fine strainer. Reserve the oil for sautéing or seasoning vegetables.

MEAT

Lamb Sausage, White Bean, and Garlic Soup | 195

Italian Sausage, Yam, and Spinach Soup | 196

Southwestern Chili Soup | 199

Parsnip, Prosciutto, and Potato Soup | 200

Belgian Beef, Beer, and Vegetable Soup | 202

Creamy Cheddar Cheese and Bacon Soup | 205

South American Pork, Peppers, and Black Bean Soup | 206

Spanish Chorizo-Garlic Soup | 209

Yellow Split Pea and Sausage Soup | 210

Louisiana Sausage and Chicken Gumbo | 213

Broccoli and Bacon Soup with Asiago Cheese Croutons | 214

Mexican Meatball Soup in Red Chile–Tomato Broth | 217

LAMB SAUSAGE, WHITE BEAN, AND GARLIC SOUP

This rustic soup reminds me of my time in Tuscany and Greece, where white bean soups are a staple of both cultures. This one is easy to make and very hearty. What gives it substance is that most of the beans are puréed along with the aromatic seasonings. The remaining beans are stirred in at the end so you can identify them.

2 teaspoons olive oil

6 ounces lamb sausage, casing removed

1 small carrot, chopped (¼ cup)

½ medium celery rib, chopped (¼ cup)

1 small or half medium onion, chopped (¼ cup)

2 large cloves garlic, chopped

1 (15½-ounce) can cannellini beans, rinsed and drained, ½ cup reserved

1¼ cups chicken stock

1½ teaspoons minced fresh rosemary leaves, plus 2 small sprigs for garnish

¼ cup drained canned petite diced tomatoes

Salt and freshly ground black pepper

2 tablespoons crumbled feta for garnish

In a medium-size saucepan, heat 1 teaspoon of the oil over medium heat. Add the sausage and sauté until the pieces are no longer pink, stirring often and breaking them into small pieces with a wooden spatula. Using a slotted spoon, remove the sausage and set aside.

Pour in the remaining teaspoon of oil and heat. Add the carrot, celery, and onion and sauté until softened, about 3 minutes, stirring often. Add the garlic and cook for 30 seconds. Add 1 cup of the stock and the minced rosemary and stir up any browned bits.

Scrape the mixture into the jar of an electric blender, add the remaining stock, and purée until smooth. Return the purée to the saucepan, stir in the reserved sausage, the remaining cannellini beans, tomatoes, and additional stock, if needed. Season to taste with salt and pepper. Ladle into bowls, sprinkle a little feta in the center, add the rosemary sprigs, and serve.

ITALIAN SAUSAGE, YAM, AND SPINACH SOUP

This stick-to-your-ribs soup is a colorful pick-me-up on bleak days.
You can make it vegetarian by substituting veggie sausages or tofu and using
vegetable broth in place of chicken stock.

2 cups peeled and roughly chopped
yams (about 9 ounces)

2 cups chicken stock

1 tablespoon fragrant olive or
vegetable oil

1 hot or sweet Italian sausage
(about 4½ ounces), casing
removed

2 large cloves garlic, minced

1½ teaspoons mild or spicy
curry powder

¼ teaspoon ground cardamom

1 tablespoon finely chopped
oil-packed sun-dried tomatoes

½ teaspoon light brown sugar

⅓ cup light cream or half-and-half

Salt and freshly ground black
pepper

2 cups baby spinach leaves (about
1½ ounces)

In a small saucepan, combine the yam with enough stock to cover. Cover the pan and gently boil until tender, about 12 minutes.

Meanwhile, combine the oil and sausage in a medium-size saucepan and cook over medium-high heat until the meat is lightly browned, chopping it into pieces with a spatula. Using a slotted spoon, remove the sausage to a plate, leaving any fat in the pan. Stir in the garlic, curry powder, and cardamom and cook until the garlic is translucent, about 30 seconds.

When the yam is tender, pour it and the stock into the pan with the garlic and seasonings, stirring up any browned cooking bits. Scrape the mixture into a food processor and purée until almost smooth. Return the mixture to the saucepan along with the sausage, sun-dried tomatoes, and sugar. Stir in any remaining stock if needed and the light cream; season to taste with salt and pepper.

Heat over medium-high heat, stir in the spinach leaves, and simmer briefly until the spinach is just wilted, 2–3 minutes. Ladle into bowls and serve.

Masa Harina

Made from corn kernels soaked in boiling water and lye, they are then dried and ground, Masa Harina is a popular way to thicken Mexican stews and soups. To avoid lumps, blend the masa with a little warm liquid into a smooth paste before adding it to the hot soup. The soup should thicken almost immediately.

SOUTHWESTERN CHILI SOUP

My kids and I have eaten chili for decades. Over the years, the heat level increased with their height. To tame the taste in this somewhat spicy, soupy version, omit the jalapeño and red pepper flakes. It is thickened with masa harina (see the sidebar). The soup can be dressed up with "all the fixin's"—including grated Jack or Cheddar cheese, sliced olives, pickled jalapeños, and diced avocado. You can also make it with ground turkey.

1 tablespoon canola or other vegetable oil

1 medium onion, diced (½ cup)

2 large cloves garlic, finely chopped

½ jalapeño pepper, seeds and membranes removed, minced (optional)

4 ounces lean ground beef

4 ounces lean ground pork

2 teaspoons ground chile powder

1 teaspoon ground cumin

½ teaspoon dried oregano

1¼ cups beef stock

½ cup crushed canned tomatoes

1 teaspoon Worcestershire sauce

Pinch red pepper flakes (optional)

½ green bell pepper, diced (about ¼ cup)

Salt and freshly ground black pepper

½ cup canned red kidney beans, rinsed and drained

2 teaspoons masa harina or fine cornmeal, mixed with a little water into a smooth paste (see the sidebar)

2 tablespoons sour cream for garnish (optional)

2 tablespoons chopped cilantro leaves or sliced scallions

In a medium-size saucepan, heat the oil over medium heat. Stir in the onion and sauté until tender, 3–4 minutes. Stir in the garlic and jalapeño and cook for an additional 30 seconds.

Add the ground meats and continue cooking until they are no longer pink, about 4–5 minutes. Stir in the chile powder, cumin, and oregano. Add the stock, tomatoes, Worcestershire sauce, red pepper flakes if using, bell pepper, and salt and pepper to taste. Bring to a boil, reduce the heat to medium-low, cover, and simmer for 30 minutes, stirring occasionally.

Stir in the kidney beans and masa harina and heat through. Taste to adjust the seasonings. Ladle into bowls, add a dollop of sour cream, the cilantro or scallions, and serve with your choice of garnishes.

PARSNIP, PROSCIUTTO, AND POTATO SOUP

Parsnips always make me think of snowy winter nights when I am happy to be inside with friends. This robust soup would be a perfect antidote to the cold. Here the roots are sweated in a little butter along with onion and celery, then puréed with chicken stock. Once cooked, parsnips' mildly sweet taste is nicely balanced with tiny cubes of crisp prosciutto and sautéed potatoes. The soup is enriched with just a little light cream. Served with a salad, it makes a satisfying lunch or even a light supper.

1½ tablespoons extra-virgin olive oil

2 cups finely chopped parsnips (about 7 ounces)

1 medium onion, finely chopped (½ cup)

½ medium celery rib, finely chopped (¼ cup)

1 clove garlic, minced

1 small Yukon Gold or other waxy potato cut into ¼-inch cubes (½ cup)

¼ cup finely diced prosciutto

1½ cups chicken stock

4–5 tablespoons light cream (optional)

1 tablespoon finely chopped flat-leaf parsley, plus a couple of leaves for garnish

Salt

In a medium-size saucepan, heat 1 tablespoon of the oil over medium heat. Add the parsnips, onion, and celery. Cover tightly, reduce the heat to low, and sweat until the parsnips are tender, 13–15 minutes, stirring occasionally. Stir in the garlic and cook for 30 seconds.

Meanwhile, in a small skillet, heat the remaining ½ tablespoon of oil over medium-high heat until hot. Add the potato cubes and sauté until golden and crisp, 3–4 minutes, turning often. Stir in the prosciutto and cook until crisp; keep the mixture warm.

Add the stock to the parsnips, stirring up any browned bits. Scrape into the jar of an electric blender and purée until smooth. Return the soup to the saucepan. Stir in the light cream if using, or a little more stock, and parsley. Heat until hot. Season to taste with salt, ladle into two bowls, spoon the sautéed potatoes and prosciutto into the soup, add the remaining parsley leaves, and serve.

BELGIAN BEEF, BEER, AND VEGETABLE SOUP

This warming soup of beef and vegetables simmered in Belgian beer is perfect for a chilly night. Not only do Belgians have plenty of blustery evenings, they also have hundreds of exceptional beers to drink and use in cooking. While in Brussels, I sampled many wonderful dishes made with local beers. You could also use this recipe to make a terrific boeuf bourguignon soup by using Burgundy wine rather than beer.

1 tablespoon canola or other vegetable oil

7 ounces beef round, trimmed, cut into ¾-inch cubes, and blotted dry

1 tablespoon all-purpose flour

Salt and freshly ground black pepper

2 slices bacon, cut crosswise into ½-inch strips

1 medium onion, chopped (½ cup)

1 large clove garlic, finely chopped

½ cup full-flavored Belgian or other beer

1½ cups beef stock

1 tablespoon tomato paste

1 medium carrot, thickly sliced (½ cup)

1 cup thickly sliced cremini mushrooms (about 3 ounces)

1 sprig flat-leaf parsley, plus 2 tablespoons chopped parsley for garnish

1 teaspoon dried thyme leaves

½ bay leaf

Salt and freshly ground pepper

½ cup frozen pearl onions

½ cup frozen petite peas

In a medium-size saucepan, heat the oil over medium-high heat. Add the beef and brown on all sides, about 3 minutes, taking care not to crowd the pieces. Sprinkle the flour on the meat, turn to coat the pieces, and transfer them to a bowl. Season with salt and pepper and set aside.

Add the bacon to the pan and cook over medium heat for 3 minutes to melt some of the fat, stirring frequently. Stir in the chopped onion and sauté until golden. Stir in the garlic and cook for 30 seconds. Pour in the beer and stir up any browned bits. Add the stock, tomato paste, carrots, mushrooms, parsley sprig, thyme, and bay leaf. Return the meat to the pan and bring the liquid to a boil.

Cover the pan, reduce the heat, and simmer until the meat is tender, at least 35 minutes. Season to taste with salt and pepper. Remove the bay leaf, stir in the pearl onions and peas, and simmer until the vegetables are cooked and the meat is very tender, about 7 minutes. Ladle into bowls, sprinkle on the remaining parsley, and serve.

CREAMY CHEDDAR CHEESE AND BACON SOUP

Grilled cheese and bacon sandwiches are a wonderful indulgence that appeals to all ages. Kathleen Sanderson, one of the founding teachers at my cooking school in Kings Super Market, turned the combo into this deliciously creamy soup with the bacon crumbled in it. (For fun, you can also serve this in mugs, with whole pieces of bacon as a stand in for the spoon!) You might stir in sautéed wild mushrooms deglazed with sherry, julienned sun-dried tomatoes, or a splash of Belgian beer at the end when the soup is hot. For a colorful and healthful addition, add blanched broccoli florets.

6 slices bacon (about 6 ounces)

Unsalted butter

5 tablespoons all-purpose flour

4 cups chicken or vegetable stock, heated

1½ cups grated sharp Cheddar cheese (about 4 ounces)

1½ teaspoons dried mustard

1 teaspoon Worcestershire sauce

Tabasco sauce

Salt and white pepper

In a large skillet, cook the bacon over medium-low heat until browned and very crisp. Remove, blot on paper towels, and crumble.

Strain the bacon fat into a medium-size saucepan, adding enough butter to measure 3 tablespoons total, and heat over medium heat. Whisk in the flour and cook until it becomes a pale golden color, 3–4 minutes, stirring constantly with a silicon scraper. Slowly whisk in the hot stock and bring to a boil. Reduce the heat and simmer for 15–20 minutes.

Add the bacon and Cheddar cheese and stir until the cheese has melted. Add the mustard, Worcestershire sauce, and Tabasco sauce. Season to taste with salt and pepper, ladle into bowls, and serve.

SOUTH AMERICAN PORK, PEPPERS, AND BLACK BEAN SOUP

Traveling in South America, I found cashew nuts—which are native to Brazil—used in several unique stews and dishes. In this soup, cubes of pork, bell pepper, poblano chiles, and black beans are simmered in an aromatic broth thickened with cashew nut butter. Sixteenth-century Portuguese sailors introduced the nuts to India. (In Cauliflower-Cashew Soup with Pomegranate Seeds, on page 53, finely ground raw cashews are used as a creamy thickener.) You could serve this soup with some rice, as well.

1½ tablespoons canola or other vegetable oil

6 ounces pork tenderloin, cut into ¾-inch cubes, blotted dry

Salt and freshly ground black pepper

1 medium onion, chopped (½ cup)

½ cup *each* chopped red and green bell pepper

½ medium celery rib, chopped (¼ cup)

3 tablespoons finely diced poblano chile (see the sidebar)

2 large cloves garlic, minced

1 tablespoon smoked paprika or *Pimentón de la Vera*

1 teaspoon ground cumin

1½–1¾ cups beef or chicken stock

⅓ cup rinsed and drained canned black beans

¼ cup cashew or peanut butter

½ cup thinly sliced scallions, including light green parts, for garnish

In a medium-size saucepan, heat 1 tablespoon of the oil over medium-high heat. Add the pork and brown on all sides, 2–3 minutes, stirring often. Using a slotted spoon, remove the meat to a dish and season generously with salt and pepper.

Add the remaining oil to the pan along with the onion, bell peppers, celery, poblano chiles, and sauté until wilted, about 5 minutes. Stir in the garlic and cook for 30 seconds. Return the meat to the pan, sprinkle on the paprika and cumin, and stir in 1½ cups of the stock. Bring the liquid to a boil, stir in the black beans and cashew butter. Lower the heat and simmer until the pork is tender, about 10 minutes. Taste to adjust the flavors and add the remaining stock, if needed. Sprinkle with scallions and serve.

Poblano Chiles

Poblanos are dark green chiles with a mild but rich flavor. They're frequently used for chiles rellenos. Generally about 4–5 inches long, they taper from top to bottom in a triangular shape. In their dried state they're known as ancho or mulato chiles. Poblanos are also used in the Salmon and Corn Chowder (page 153).

SPANISH CHORIZO-GARLIC SOUP

Garlic never tasted so mild as it does in this delectable Spanish-style soup in which slow cooking tames every bit of its assertive bite. Accented with tasty chorizo and a pinch of smoky red pepper, or Pimentón de la Vera, the results are very tasty. With packages of peeled garlic cloves available in supermarkets, making this dish is far easier than it once was.

1 tablespoon fragrant extra-virgin olive oil

1 tablespoon unsalted butter

2 large onions, chopped (1¾ cups)

1 cup peeled garlic cloves

2 sprigs flat-leaf parsley

1 sprig fresh thyme

⅛ teaspoon black peppercorns

½ bay leaf

2½ cups chicken stock

¾ cups torn pieces of stale French or country bread

¾ cup light cream

¼–½ teaspoon sweet Pimentón de la Vera or smoked paprika

Salt

2 ounces Spanish chorizo, casing removed, cut into small cubes

In a medium-size saucepan, heat the oil and butter over low heat. Add the onion and garlic and sauté until the garlic is tender and the onion is lightly browned, about 30 minutes, covering the pan for at least the last 10 minutes so they don't burn.

Tie the parsley, thyme, peppercorns, and bay leaf together in two layers of cheesecloth. Add the seasonings along with the stock and bread to the pot and bring to a boil. Adjust the heat down and simmer until the bread begins to fall apart, 10–15 minutes. Remove the herbs and discard.

Transfer the soup to the jar of an electric blender and purée until smooth. Return the mixture to the saucepan, stir in the cream, Pimentón de la Vera, and salt to taste. Add the chorizo and simmer until heated through. Ladle into bowls and serve with a little pimentón sprinkled on top.

YELLOW SPLIT PEA AND SAUSAGE SOUP

Split pea soup made with either yellow or green peas is another family favorite.
Meat eaters will like this version, with spicy, smoked Cajun-style andouille sausage.
(Use extra sausages in the Louisiana Sausage and Chicken Gumbo recipe on page 213.)
For kids of all ages, you could even use hot dogs. The vegetarian recipe is on page 112.

1 tablespoon canola or other vegetable oil

1 small carrot, chopped (⅓ cup)

½ medium-large celery rib, chopped (⅓ cup)

1 small onion, chopped (⅓ cup)

⅔ cup yellow split peas, sorted and rinsed

2 cups chicken stock

2 cups water

½ teaspoon dried thyme leaves

½ bay leaf

1 (4½-ounce) andouille sausage, cut into ¼-inch slices or diced

1 tablespoon chopped flat-leaf parsley

Salt and freshly ground black pepper

Pumpernickel-Parmesan Croutons (page 114), if desired

In a medium-size saucepan, heat the oil over medium heat. Stir in the carrot, celery, and onion; cover the pan and sweat over medium-low heat until the vegetables are soft, about 10 minutes, stirring occasionally.

Add the peas, stock, half of the water, thyme, and bay leaf. Bring the mixture to a boil, cover, and reduce the heat so the liquid is simmering. Cook until the peas are very tender, at least 1 hour.

Remove the bay leaf, scrape the mixture into a food processor, and pulse until chunky-smooth. Return the mixture to the pan, add the sausage and enough of the remaining water to achieve a soupy consistency. Stir in the parsley and simmer until the sausage is hot. Season to taste with salt and pepper and serve with croutons if desired.

Filé Gumbo

Filé gumbo is a hallmark of Creole cooking. The dusky green seasoning, made from the dried, ground leaves of the sassafras tree, adds flavor and helps thicken the gumbo, as well. Tabasco sauce is another Louisiana native.

LOUISIANA SAUSAGE AND CHICKEN GUMBO

Spicy gumbo is the legacy of New Orleans' Cajun and Creole cooks. Filé gumbo (see the sidebar) and sliced okra thicken the broth and impart the distinctive character associated with the soup. While many gumbo recipes start with a roux, flour cooked with fat until copper brown and then mixed with stock, I prefer this hearty main-course soup without that additional thickener. And while many gumbo lovers demand white rice with it, I make it an option.

1 tablespoon canola or other vegetable oil

⅓ cup diced celery

⅓ cup diced onion

⅓ cup seeded and diced red or green bell pepper

4 ounces boneless, skinless chicken thighs, well trimmed and cut into 1-inch pieces

2 large cloves garlic, minced

1½ cups chicken stock

¾ cup drained canned diced tomatoes

½ teaspoon filé gumbo

½ teaspoon dried oregano

½ bay leaf

5–6 pieces of okra, cut into ¼-inch slices

3 tablespoons coarsely chopped flat-leaf parsley

3 ounces spicy sausage, preferably andouille, quartered lengthwise and cut into ½-inch slices

Salt and coarsely ground black pepper

Tabasco sauce

¼ cup raw long-grain rice (optional)

1 teaspoon red wine vinegar

In a medium-size saucepan, heat the oil over medium heat. Add the celery, onion, and bell pepper and sauté until crisp tender, about 4–5 minutes. Stir in the chicken and cook until the outside is no longer pink, 2–3 minutes, turning frequently. Add the garlic and cook for 30 seconds.

Add the stock, tomatoes, filé gumbo, oregano, and bay leaf. Bring the liquid to a boil, stirring up any brown cooking bits, then reduce the heat, partially cover, and simmer for 15 minutes, stirring occasionally. Stir in the okra and parsley and continue cooking until the okra is almost tender, about 15 minutes. Stir in the andouille and continue cooking until the sausage is hot and the okra is tender, about 5 minutes. Season to taste with salt, pepper, and Tabasco sauce.

While the soup simmers, cook the rice according to package directions until tender, about 20 minutes, if serving.

Turn off the heat under the soup, remove the bay leaf, stir in the vinegar, and let the soup stand for a minute. If serving rice, add a mound in the middle of each soup bowl. Ladle the gumbo over the rice and serve piping hot.

BROCCOLI AND BACON SOUP WITH ASIAGO CHEESE CROUTONS

Bacon adds its unique taste to this fragrant, vibrant green soup that takes almost no effort. For the croutons, slices of bread (I use whole grain) are brushed with rendered bacon fat and grilled with shredded Asiago cheese. As a final garnish, crumbled bacon is drizzled over each steaming bowl.

2 strips bacon, cut in half crosswise

1 medium-size bunch broccoli

½ tablespoon vegetable oil or rendered bacon fat

1 small onion, chopped (⅓ cup)

1 clove garlic, finely chopped

2¼ cups chicken stock

⅓ cup half-and-half or light cream

½ teaspoon ground cardamom

½ teaspoon ground coriander

¼ teaspoon ground nutmeg

Salt and freshly ground black pepper

2 thin slices whole grain bread

½ cup shredded Asiago or other flavorful cheese

In a skillet, cook the bacon over medium heat until crisp. Remove, blot on paper towels, and crumble. Strain and reserve the fat.

Cut off about 1 cup of tiny broccoli florets, blanch in boiling water until tender, about 2 minutes, drain under cold water, blot dry, and set aside. Roughly chop the remaining broccoli.

In a medium-size saucepan, heat the oil over medium heat. Add the onion and sauté until golden and soft, 3–4 minutes, stirring often. Add the garlic and cook for 30 seconds. Pour in the stock, add the broccoli, and gently boil until completely tender, about 8 minutes. Transfer to the jar of an electric blender and purée until smooth.

Return the soup to the pan, stir in the half-and-half, cardamom, coriander, nutmeg, and reserved broccoli florets. Season with salt and pepper to taste and simmer until hot.

Meanwhile, lightly brush both sides of the sliced bread with the reserved bacon fat. Place a bread slice in a small skillet, drizzle the cheese over it, cover with the second slice, and cook over low heat until golden, about 2 minutes; turn and cook the second side until golden and the cheese is melted. Remove and let stand for a few minutes. Using a serrated bread knife, cut off the crusts, and cut the bread into 1-inch squares. Serve the soup with the croutons and with the bacon sprinkled on top.

MEXICAN MEATBALL SOUP IN RED CHILE–TOMATO BROTH

When most people think of meatballs, they think Italian. But this soup shows that albondigas (Mexican meatballs) in soup is also a beloved traditional dish. Vegetables, meatballs, and cheese are spooned in the bottom of bowls and boiling hot broth ladled over them. As with many Mexican soups, this one may be served as a starter or main course. Soups are usually served with warm corn tortillas on the side. This recipe is adapted from one by Ivy Stark, executive chef of Dos Caminos restaurants.

For the meatballs:

1½ tablespoons canola or other vegetable oil, plus oil to grease the pan

1 small or half medium onion, finely diced (¼ cup)

1 clove garlic, chopped

1 small tomatillo, husked and diced

1 serrano chile, seeds removed if desired, chopped

¼ pound ground beef

¼ pound ground pork

1 large egg, lightly beaten

¼ cup Japanese breadcrumbs (panko) or Italian breadcrumbs

2 tablespoons chopped cilantro leaves

Coarse salt and freshly ground black pepper

To make the meatballs, begin by heating a large, heavy skillet over medium heat. Add ½ tablespoon of the oil and the onion and gently sauté until translucent, about 3 minutes, stirring occasionally. Add the garlic and sauté for 30 seconds. Stir in the tomatillos and serrano chile, lower the heat to medium-low, and sauté until the mixture is reduced, about 5 minutes. Set aside to cool.

Preheat the oven to 350 degrees F. Lightly grease a baking sheet.

In a large bowl, combine the ground meats. Make a well in the center, add the tomatillo mixture, egg, breadcrumbs, and 2 tablespoons cilantro; season with about ½ teaspoon of salt and pepper to taste and gently mix until combined. Roll the mixture into 1-inch balls and bake on the baking sheet until just cooked through, 7–8 minutes. Remove and set aside to cool.

To make the soup, heat a heavy-bottomed pan over medium-high heat. Add the olive oil and onion and sauté until translucent, about 3 minutes. Add the garlic and sauté for 30 seconds. Stir in the tomatoes and cook for 2 minutes. Scrape the mixture along with the chipotles into the jar of an electric blender and purée until smooth.

For the soup:

1 tablespoon olive oil

1 small or half medium onion, coarsely chopped (¼ cup)

1 clove garlic, coarsely chopped

2 plum tomatoes, quartered

1-2 canned chipotle chiles en adobo, according to taste

2 cups chicken stock

1 bay leaf

1 tablespoon chopped fresh hoja santa leaves (available at Hispanic markets) *or* chopped fennel leaves

¼ teaspoon dried oregano, preferably Mexican

Kosher salt

¼ cup diced chayote, blanched (see the sidebar)

¼ cup roasted corn kernels cut from the cob or cooked defrosted corn

¼ pound *queso fresco*, cubed, for garnish (see the sidebar)

2 tablespoons chopped cilantro leaves for garnish

Pour the mixture into a medium-size saucepan, add the chicken stock, bay leaves, hoja santa, oregano, and salt to taste; bring to a simmer over medium heat. Reduce the heat to low and gently simmer for 15 minutes. Strain into a clean pan and keep hot.

In a large skillet over medium-high heat, heat the remaining 1 tablespoon of oil from the meatball ingredients. Add the meatballs to the pan in batches, taking care not to crowd them; brown them on all sides and cook until heated through, 2–3 minutes.

Divide the chayote and corn among large, warm soup bowls. Spoon 3–4 meatballs into each bowl and crumble a little queso fresco in, as well. Ladle the hot broth into each bowl, garnish with the remaining 2 tablespoons of cilantro, and serve.

Queso Fresco and Chayote

Queso fresco is a fresh, unaged cow's milk cheese produced throughout Mexico. It's used as a table cheese, crumbled as a topping, or as a stuffing for chiles or quesadillas because it melts well. It has a pleasant acidity and creaminess and is similar to queso blanco.

Chayote, also known as alligator pear, is a mild-tasting, squash-like green fruit that resembles a pear. It is native to Mexico. Remove its firm skin with a sharp paring knife or vegetable peeler before cutting it up.

ACKNOWLEDGMENTS

Thanks to my exceptional editor Ann Treistman for helping me to capture the essence of soup making for today's cooks.

I'm very grateful to my friends who shared recipes, tested and retested them, offered helpful suggestions, and gave me abundant encouragement:
Louise Aaronson,
Lidia Bastianich,
Karen Berk,
Sarah and Glenn Collins,
Jessica Craig-Smith,
Pam Harding,
Terry Holler,
Sally, Gene, and Leigh Kofke,
Susan Kolsby and Eddy Kelly,
Bob Lape,
Mark Melton,
Bruce Robertson and Lynne Van Auken,
Bette Shifman and David Burfoot,
Marcie Sweigert
Rick Waln,
Carole Walter,
Guzin Yalin,
and Mike O'Donnell, the manager of Fairway Market in Harlem, and many of his staff, for so much help.

On the technical side, my thanks go to:

Photographer Noah Fecks for his passion and creativity in capturing the varied textures and colors of these soups, and making them look good enough to eat.

Greta Titelman, the ultimate executive assistant, who kept the show (and Noah) on track.

LeAnna Weller Smith for her exciting contemporary design.

Sarah Bennett—an intern with a promising future based on her enthusiastic assistance during the photo shoot.

Jill Mason for her copyediting

Anya Frankenberg for her artistic makeup

Rosa Herrera for keeping my kitchen so organized and clean.

Finally, I could write an ode to Joy Strang for her tireless and enthusiastic efforts during the writing of this book. Always excited by the results and willing to help me tweak recipes that needed improvement, Joy, I feel so blessed to have had you on my team.

INDEX

A

Adobo sauce, about, 40
Almond(s)
  -Broccoli Soup with
    Gruyère Crisps, 130
  -Garlic Soup,
    Andalusian, 54
  Ground, 143
  Spanish Lobster
    and Sea Scallop
    Chowder, 143
  Toasted, 130
Andalusian Garlic-
  Almond Soup, 54
Apple cider
  Peach Soup with Sugar-
    Glazed Blackberries,
    32
  Wild Mushroom Soup,
    87
Apple(s)
  Celery Root, Chestnut,
    and Gorgonzola
    Soup, 132
  -Rutabaga Soup,
    Spiced, 88
  Wild Mushroom Soup,
    87
Asiago
  Cheese Croutons, 214
  and Rosemary Crostini,
    119
Avocado(s)
  Hass, about, 47
  Mexican Chicken
    Tortilla Soup, 179
  Shrimp Posole, 154
  Soup, Puréed, with
    Guacamole
    Toppings, 47

B

Bacon
  and Broccoli Soup

with Asiago Cheese
  Croutons, 214
and Cheddar Cheese
  Soup, Creamy, 205
Clam, Potato, and Kale
  Soup with, 144
Gascon Duck Confit
  and Vegetable Soup,
  190
White Bean, Vegetable,
  and Sun-Dried
  Tomato Soup, 118
Balsamic-Glazed
  Butternut Squash and
  Goat Cheese, Lentil
  Soup with, 107
Barley
  -Mushroom Soup,
    Nanny Annie's, 122
  Scottish Cock-a-Leekie
    Soup, 180
  -Turkey and Spinach
    Soup, 124
Basil
  Chilled Summer Tomato
    Soup with Pesto, 43
  Cream, Salted, Spicy
    Roasted Tomato–Red
    Pepper Soup with, 77
  Double Chickpea–Two
    Tomato Soup, 121
  Pesto, Bruce's
    Homemade, 44
  Pistou, 70
  Provençal Tomato-
    Fennel Soup with
    Saffron, 74
Bean(s)
  Black, Pork, and
    Peppers Soup, South
    American, 206
  Black, Pumpkin, and
    Tomato Soup, 117
  Crunchy Chickpeas, 58
  Double Chickpea–Two

Tomato Soup, 121
Green, –Mushroom
  Soup with Frizzled
  Onion Strings, 68
Green Vegetable Soup
  with Pistou, 70
Minted Spiced Green
  Pea Soup with
  Crunchy Chickpeas,
  57
Mom's Minestrone, 93
Moroccan Tomato-
  Chickpea Soup, 128
Quick Vegetable Soup,
  25
"Silk Purse" Roasted
  Leftover Root
  Vegetable Soup, 95
Southwestern Chili
  Soup, 199
-Turkey-Vegetable
  Soup, Hearty, 127
White, Lamb Sausage,
  and Garlic Soup, 195
White, Vegetable, and
  Sun-Dried Tomato
  Soup, 118
Beef
  Belgian Beer, and
    Vegetable Soup, 202
  Mexican Meatball Soup
    in Red Chile–Tomato
    Broth, 216–17
  Southwestern Chili
    Soup, 199
Beer, Belgian, Beef, and
  Vegetable Soup, 202
Beet
  Borscht, Blueberry-
    Pomegranate, 31
  Roasted, Soup with
    Dukkah, Yogurt, and
    Black Currant, 48
Belgian Beef, Beer, and
  Vegetable Soup, 202

Blackberries, Sugar-
Glazed, Peach Soup
with, 32
Black Currant, Dukkah,
and Yogurt, Roasted
Beet Soup with, 48
Blenders, 16
Blueberry(ies)
-Pomegranate Beet
Borscht, 31
and Toasted Coconut,
Pineapple Soup with,
35
Bok Choy
Gascon Duck Confit
and Vegetable Soup,
190
Japanese Chicken and
Noodle Soup, 172
Mom's Minestrone, 93
Tofu, Shiitakes, and
Soba Noodles, Miso
Soup with, 81
Borscht, Blueberry-
Pomegranate Beet, 31
Breads
Asiago and Rosemary
Crostini, 119
Asiago Cheese
Croutons, 214
Crostini for Onion-Leek
Soup, 90
Mini Cheese Triangles,
79
Pumpernickel-Parmesan
Croutons, 114
Broccoli
-Almond Soup with
Gruyère Crisps, 130
and Bacon Soup with
Asiago Cheese
Croutons, 214
Broths, 20
Bruce's Homemade Basil
Pesto, 44
Buttermilk
Chilled Fire-Roasted
Tomato Bisque, 40

Frizzled Onion Strings,
69
Morello Cherry Soup
with Candied Ginger
and Fennel, 36

C

Carrot(s)
cutting or chopping, 23
-Ginger Soup, Thai,
100
-Ginger Soup with
Chèvre, 67
Hearty Turkey-
Vegetable-Bean
Soup, 127
Japanese Chicken and
Noodle Soup, 172
Nonna's Rice and
Potato Soup, 84
"Silk Purse" Roasted
Leftover Root
Vegetable Soup, 95
Cashew butter
South American Pork,
Peppers, and Black
Bean Soup, 206
Cashew-Cauliflower
Soup with
Pomegranate Seeds,
53
Cauliflower
-Cashew Soup with
Pomegranate Seeds,
53
Hearty Turkey-
Vegetable-Bean
Soup, 127
Celery
"Silk Purse" Roasted
Leftover Root
Vegetable Soup, 95
slicing or chopping, 23
Celery Root
about, 132
Chestnut, and
Gorgonzola Soup,
132

Chayote
about, 217
Mexican Meatball Soup
in Red Chile–Tomato
Broth, 216–17
Cheddar
Cheese and Bacon
Soup, Creamy, 205
Rainy Day Tomato
Bisque with Mini
Cheese Triangles, 79
Cheese
Asiago, Croutons, 214
Asiago and Rosemary
Crostini, 119
Bruce's Homemade
Basil Pesto, 44
Carrot-Ginger Soup
with Chèvre, 67
Celery Root, Chestnut,
and Gorgonzola
Soup, 132
Cheddar, and Bacon
Soup, Creamy, 205
Crostini for Onion-Leek
Soup, 90
Goat, and Balsamic-
Glazed Butternut
Squash, Lentil Soup
with, 107
Gruyère Crisps, 131
Lamb Sausage, White
Bean, and Garlic
Soup, 195
Lemon-Parsley Pesto,
151
Mexican Chicken
Tortilla Soup, 179
Mexican Meatball Soup
in Red Chile–Tomato
Broth, 216–17
Mom's Minestrone, 93
Nonna's Rice and
Potato Soup, 84
Pistou, 70
Pumpernickel-Parmesan
Croutons, 114
queso fresco, about, 217

Triangles, Mini, Rainy Day Tomato Bisque with, 79
Turkish Eggplant Soup, 96
Watermelon Gazpacho Soup, 39
Cherry, Morello, Soup with Candied Ginger and Fennel, 36
Chestnut, Celery Root, and Gorgonzola Soup, 132
Chèvre, Carrot-Ginger Soup with, 67
Chicken
  and Coconut Milk Soup, Thai, 185
  Laksa, Malaysian, 175
  Lemon, and Rice Soup, Greek, 165
  Noodle Soup, Far Better Than Canned, 166
  and Noodle Soup, Japanese, 172
  parts, cooking with, 167
  and Sausage Gumbo, Louisiana, 213
  Scottish Cock-a-Leekie Soup, 180
  Soup, Circassian, 186
  Soup, Jamaican Jerk, with Coconut, Plantains, and Peppers, 176
  Soup for the Soul, 168
  Tortilla Soup, Mexican, 179
  -Vegetable and Orzo Soup, 171
  West African Peanut Soup with, 137
  whole, buying, 167
Chickpea(s)
  Crunchy, 58
  Crunchy, Minted Spiced Green Pea Soup with, 57

Double, –Two Tomato Soup, 121
Hearty Turkey-Vegetable-Bean Soup, 127
Mom's Minestrone, 93
"Silk Purse" Roasted Leftover Root Vegetable Soup, 95
-Tomato Soup, Moroccan, 128
Chile(s)
  Chilled Fire-Roasted Tomato Bisque, 40
  Gazpacho, 60
  Leftover Turkey and Tomatillo Soup, 188
  Malaysian Chicken Laksa, 175
  Mexican Chicken Tortilla Soup, 179
  poblano, about, 206
  Puréed Avocado Soup with Guacamole Toppings, 47
  Red, –Tomato Broth, Mexican Meatball Soup in, 216–17
  Salmon and Corn Chowder, 153
  Shrimp Posole, 154
  "Silk Purse" Roasted Leftover Root Vegetable Soup, 95
  South American Pork, Peppers, and Black Bean Soup, 206
  Southwestern Chili Soup, 199
  Thai Chicken and Coconut Milk Soup, 185
  Thai Coconut-Mussel Soup, 148
  Watermelon Gazpacho Soup, 39
Chile-Spiced Pumpkin Seeds, 115

Chili Soup, Southwestern, 199
Chilled soups
  Andalusian Garlic-Almond Soup, 54
  Blueberry-Pomegranate Beet Borscht, 31
  Cauliflower-Cashew Soup with Pomegranate Seeds, 53
  Chilled Fire-Roasted Tomato Bisque, 40
  Chilled Strawberry-Ginger Soup, 28
  Chilled Summer Tomato Soup with Pesto, 43
  Cucumber-Watercress Soup with Diced Tomatoes, 61
  Curried Cucumber and Scallion Soup, 51
  Gazpacho, 60
  Minted Spiced Green Pea Soup with Crunchy Chickpeas, 57
  Morello Cherry Soup with Candied Ginger and Fennel, 36
  Peach Soup with Sugar-Glazed Blackberries, 32
  Pineapple Soup with Blueberries and Toasted Coconut, 35
  Puréed Avocado Soup with Guacamole Toppings, 47
  Roasted Beet Soup with Dukkah, Yogurt, and Black Currant, 48
  Watermelon Gazpacho Soup, 39
Chinese Noodle Soup with Shrimp, 161
Chorizo
  and Red Lentil Soup,

Spanish, 108
Spanish, –Garlic Soup, 209
Spanish vs. Mexican, 108
Chowder
  Salmon and Corn, 153
  Seafood, 158
Chunky Leek, Potato, and Tomato Soup, 76
Cilantro
  Chinese Noodle Soup with Shrimp, 161
  Gazpacho, 60
  Leftover Turkey and Tomatillo Soup, 188
  Malaysian Chicken Laksa, 175
  Mexican Chicken Tortilla Soup, 179
  Mexican Meatball Soup in Red Chile–Tomato Broth, 216–17
  Moroccan Tomato-Chickpea Soup, 128
  Puréed Avocado Soup with Guacamole Toppings, 47
  Shrimp Posole, 154
  "Silk Purse" Roasted Leftover Root Vegetable Soup, 95
  Southwestern Chili Soup, 199
  Thai Chicken and Coconut Milk Soup, 185
  West African Peanut Soup with Chicken, 137
Circassian Chicken Soup, 186
Clam, Potato, and Kale Soup with Bacon, 144
Cock-a-Leekie Soup, Scottish, 180
Coconut
  Plantains, and Peppers,

Jamaican Jerk Chicken Soup with, 176
  -Pumpkin Soup, Curried, 98
Toasted, and Blueberries, Pineapple Soup with, 35
water, about, 98
Coconut Milk
  Cauliflower-Cashew Soup with Pomegranate Seeds, 53
  and Chicken Soup, Thai, 185
  cooking with, 98
  Curried Pumpkin-Coconut Soup, 98
  Jamaican Jerk Chicken Soup with Coconut, Plantains, and Peppers, 176
  Malaysian Chicken Laksa, 175
  Pineapple Soup with Blueberries and Toasted Coconut, 35
  Thai Carrot-Ginger Soup, 100
  Thai Coconut-Mussel Soup, 148
  Thai Mango-Shrimp Soup, 157
Coriander
  Dukkah, 49
  West African Peanut Soup with Chicken, 137
Corn
  Chicken-Vegetable and Orzo Soup, 171
  Leftover Turkey and Tomatillo Soup, 188
  Mexican Meatball Soup in Red Chile–Tomato Broth, 216–17

and Salmon Chowder, 153
  Shrimp Posole, 154
Crabmeat
  Watermelon Gazpacho Soup, 39
Cranberries
  Scottish Cock-a-Leekie Soup, 180
Creamy Cheddar Cheese and Bacon Soup, 205
Creamy Onion-Leek and Shallot Bisque, 90
Creamy Oyster Soup with Lemon-Parsley Pesto, 150
Crispy Tortilla Strips, 189
Crostini
  Asiago and Rosemary, 119
  for Onion-Leek Soup, 90
Croutons
  Asiago Cheese, 214
  Pumpernickel-Parmesan, 114
Crunchy Chickpeas, 58
Crunchy Leek Topping, 91
Cucumber(s)
  Gazpacho, 60
  and Scallion Soup, Curried, 51
  -Watercress Soup with Diced Tomatoes, 61
Curried soups
  Curried Cucumber and Scallion Soup, 51
  Curried Pumpkin-Coconut Soup, 98
  Italian Sausage, Yam, and Spinach Soup, 196
  Minted Spiced Green Pea Soup with Crunchy Chickpeas, 57
  Thai Carrot-Ginger Soup, 100

Curried soups *(continued)*
  Thai Mango-Shrimp
    Soup, 157

D

Dessert soups
  Chilled Strawberry-
    Ginger Soup, 28
  Morello Cherry Soup
    with Candied Ginger
    and Fennel, 36
  Peach Soup with Sugar-
    Glazed Blackberries,
    32
  Pineapple Soup with
    Blueberries and
    Toasted Coconut, 35
Dill
  Curried Cucumber and
    Scallion Soup, 51
  Nanny Annie's Barley-
    Mushroom Soup,
    122
  Salmon and Corn
    Chowder, 153
  Turkey-Barley and
    Spinach Soup, 124
Double Chickpea–Two
  Tomato Soup, 121
Duck Confit and
  Vegetable Soup,
  Gascon, 190
Dukkah, 49
Dukkah, Yogurt, and
  Black Currant, Roasted
  Beet Soup with, 48

E

Eggplant Soup, Turkish,
  96
Eggs
  Gascon Duck Confit
    and Vegetable Soup,
    190
  Greek Lemon Chicken
    and Rice Soup, 165
Electric blenders, 16
Equipment, 16

F

Far Better Than Canned
  Chicken Noodle Soup,
  166
Fennel
  and Candied Ginger,
    Morello Cherry Soup
    with, 36
  Crunchy Chickpeas, 58
  Dukkah, 49
  Provençal Mussel Soup,
    147
  "Silk Purse" Roasted
    Leftover Root
    Vegetable Soup, 95
  -Tomato Soup,
    Provençal, with
    Saffron, 74
Feta cheese
  Lamb Sausage, White
    Bean, and Garlic
    Soup, 195
  Turkish Eggplant Soup,
    96
  Watermelon Gazpacho
    Soup, 39
Filé gumbo, about, 212
Finnish Jerusalem
  Artichoke Soup with
  Marinated Tofu, 103
Fish
  Salmon and Corn
    Chowder, 153
  Seafood Chowder, 158
Food processors, 16
French Green Lentil
  Soup, 111
Frizzled Onion Strings, 69

G

Garlic
  -Almond Soup,
    Andalusian, 54
  Lamb Sausage, and
    White Bean Soup,
    195
  Lemon-Parsley Pesto,
    151

Pistou, 70
  Roasted, 191
  -Spanish Chorizo Soup,
    209
Garnishes
  Asiago and Rosemary
    Crostini, 119
  Bruce's Homemade
    Basil Pesto, 44
  Chile-Spiced Pumpkin
    Seeds, 115
  Crispy Tortilla Strips,
    189
  Crostini for Onion-Leek
    Soup, 90
  Crunchy Chickpeas, 58
  Crunchy Leek Topping,
    91
  Dukkah, 49
  Frizzled Onion Strings,
    69
  Gruyère Crisps, 131
  Harissa-Yogurt Drizzle,
    129
  Lemon-Parsley Pesto,
    151
  Mini Cheese Triangles,
    79
  Pistou, 70
  Pumpernickel-Parmesan
    Croutons, 114
  Salted Basil Cream, 77
  Sugar-Glazed
    Blackberries, 32
Gascon Duck Confit and
  Vegetable Soup, 190
Gazpacho, 60
Gazpacho Soup,
  Watermelon, 39
Ginger
  Candied, and Fennel,
    Morello Cherry Soup
    with, 36
  -Carrot Soup, Thai, 100
  -Carrot Soup with
    Chèvre, 67
  Chinese Noodle Soup
    with Shrimp, 161

Miso Soup with Tofu, Shiitakes, Bok Choy, and Soba Noodles, 81

Pineapple Soup with Blueberries and Toasted Coconut, 35

"Silk Purse" Roasted Leftover Root Vegetable Soup, 95

Spiced Rutabaga-Apple Soup, 88

-Strawberry Soup, Chilled, 28

Thai Mango-Shrimp Soup, 157

West African Peanut Soup with Chicken, 137

Goat Cheese and Balsamic-Glazed Butternut Squash, Lentil Soup with, 107

Gorgonzola, Celery Root, and Chestnut Soup, 132

Grains
  Greek Lemon Chicken and Rice Soup, 165
  Nanny Annie's Barley-Mushroom Soup, 122
  Nonna's Rice and Potato Soup, 84
  Scottish Cock-a-Leekie Soup, 180
  Turkey-Barley and Spinach Soup, 124

Grana Padano cheese
  Nonna's Rice and Potato Soup, 84

Grapes
  Andalusian Garlic-Almond Soup, 54

Greek Lemon Chicken and Rice Soup, 165

Green Bean–Mushroom Soup with Frizzled Onion Strings, 68

Greens. See also Spinach

Clam, Potato, and Kale Soup with Bacon, 144

Cucumber-Watercress Soup with Diced Tomatoes, 61

Kale, Potato, Tofu, and Sun-Dried Tomato Soup, 73

lacinato kale, about, 144

Radish, Soup with Toasted Hazelnuts, 139

Scallop and Kale Soup, 142

Green Vegetable Soup with Pistou, 70

Gruyère
  Crisps, 131
  Crostini for Onion-Leek Soup, 90

Gumbo, Louisiana Sausage and Chicken, 213

H

Ham
  Black Bean, Pumpkin, and Tomato Soup, 117
  Parsnip, Prosciutto, and Potato Soup, 200

Harissa-Yogurt Drizzle, 129

Hazelnuts
  Toasted, Radish Greens Soup with, 139
  Wild Mushroom Soup, 87

Hearty Turkey-Vegetable-Bean Soup, 127

Herbs. See also specific herbs
  herbes de Provence, about, 75

Hominy
  Shrimp Posole, 154

I

Italian Sausage, Yam, and Spinach Soup, 196

J

Jamaican Jerk Chicken Soup with Coconut, Plantains, and Peppers, 176

Japanese Chicken and Noodle Soup, 172

Jerusalem Artichoke Soup, Finnish, with Marinated Tofu, 103

K

Kale
  Clam, and Potato Soup with Bacon, 144
  lacinato, about, 144
  Potato, Tofu, and Sun-Dried Tomato Soup, 73
  and Scallop Soup, 142

Knives, 23

L

Lamb Sausage, White Bean, and Garlic Soup, 195

Leek(s)
  Gascon Duck Confit and Vegetable Soup, 190
  Hearty Turkey-Vegetable-Bean Soup, 127
  -Onion and Shallot Bisque, Creamy, 90
  Potato, and Tomato Soup, Chunky, 76
  Provençal Mussel Soup, 147
  Scottish Cock-a-Leekie Soup, 180
  Topping, Crunchy, 91

Leftover Turkey and Tomatillo Soup, 188

Legume, nut, and bean soups
  Black Bean, Pumpkin, and Tomato Soup, 117
  Broccoli-Almond Soup with Gruyère Crisps, 130
  Celery Root, Chestnut, and Gorgonzola Soup, 132
  Double Chickpea–Two Tomato Soup, 121
  French Green Lentil Soup, 111
  Hearty Turkey-Vegetable-Bean Soup, 127
  Lentil Soup with Balsamic-Glazed Butternut Squash and Goat Cheese, 107
  Moroccan Tomato-Chickpea Soup, 128
  Nanny Annie's Barley-Mushroom Soup, 122
  Radish Greens Soup with Toasted Hazelnuts, 139
  Spanish Red Lentil and Chorizo Soup, 108
  Turkey-Barley and Spinach Soup, 124
  Vegetarian Split Green Pea Soup, 112
  West African Peanut Soup with Chicken, 137
  White Bean, Vegetable, and Sun-Dried Tomato Soup, 118
Lemon
  Chicken and Rice Soup, Greek, 165
  Curried Cucumber and Scallion Soup, 51
  -Parsley Pesto, 151

Lemongrass
  Malaysian Chicken Laksa, 175
  preparing, for cooking, 148
  Thai Chicken and Coconut Milk Soup, 185
  Thai Coconut-Mussel Soup, 148
  Thai Mango-Shrimp Soup, 157
Lentil
  French Green, Soup, 111
  Red, and Chorizo Soup, Spanish, 108
  Soup with Balsamic-Glazed Butternut Squash and Goat Cheese, 107
Lobster and Sea Scallop Chowder, Spanish, 143
Louisiana Sausage and Chicken Gumbo, 213

M
Malaysian Chicken Laksa, 175
Mango
  cutting up, 157
  peeling, 157
  -Shrimp Soup, Thai, 157
Masa harina
  about, 198
  Southwestern Chili Soup, 199
Matzo Balls, 169
Meatball Soup, Mexican, in Red Chile–Tomato Broth, 216–17
Meat soups
  Belgian Beef, Beer, and Vegetable Soup, 202
  Broccoli and Bacon Soup with Asiago Cheese Croutons, 214

  Creamy Cheddar Cheese and Bacon Soup, 205
  Italian Sausage, Yam, and Spinach Soup, 196
  Lamb Sausage, White Bean, and Garlic Soup, 195
  Louisiana Sausage and Chicken Gumbo, 213
  Mexican Meatball Soup in Red Chile–Tomato Broth, 216–17
  Parsnip, Prosciutto, and Potato Soup, 200
  South American Pork, Peppers, and Black Bean Soup, 206
  Southwestern Chili Soup, 199
  Spanish Chorizo-Garlic Soup, 209
  Yellow Split Pea and Sausage Soup, 210
Mexican Chicken Tortilla Soup, 179
Mexican Meatball Soup in Red Chile–Tomato Broth, 216–17
Minestrone, Mom's, 93
Mini Cheese Triangles, 79
Mint
  Chilled Strawberry-Ginger Soup, 28
  French Green Lentil Soup, 111
  Malaysian Chicken Laksa, 175
  Minted Spiced Green Pea Soup with Crunchy Chickpeas, 57
  Peach Soup with Sugar-Glazed Blackberries, 32
  Watermelon Gazpacho Soup, 39

Miso
  Soup with Tofu,
    Shiitakes, Bok Choy,
    and Soba Noodles,
    81
  varieties of, 81
Mole
  buying, 65
  and Peppers, Butternut
    Squash Soup with,
    64
  store-bought, flavoring,
    65
Mom's Minestrone, 93
Morello Cherry Soup with
  Candied Ginger and
  Fennel, 36
Moroccan Tomato-
  Chickpea Soup, 128
Mushroom(s)
  baby bella or cremini,
    about, 69
  -Barley Soup, Nanny
    Annie's, 122
  Belgian Beef, Beer, and
    Vegetable Soup, 202
  Chinese Noodle Soup
    with Shrimp, 161
  –Green Bean Soup
    with Frizzled Onion
    Strings, 68
  Hearty Turkey-
    Vegetable-Bean
    Soup, 127
  Japanese Chicken and
    Noodle Soup, 172
  Miso Soup with Tofu,
    Shiitakes, Bok Choy,
    and Soba Noodles,
    81
  Mom's Minestrone, 93
  Thai Chicken and
    Coconut Milk Soup,
    185
  Wild, Soup, 87
Mussel(s)
  -Coconut Soup, Thai,
    148

Seafood Chowder, 158
Soup, Provençal, 147

N
Nanny Annie's Barley-
  Mushroom Soup, 122
Nonna's Rice and Potato
  Soup, 84
Noodle(s)
  Chicken Soup, Far
    Better Than Canned,
    166
  and Chicken Soup,
    Japanese, 172
  Chinese, Soup with
    Shrimp, 161
  Malaysian Chicken
    Laksa, 175
  Soba, Tofu, Shiitakes,
    and Bok Choy, Miso
    Soup with, 81
Nuts. See also Almond(s);
  Pine nuts
  Cauliflower-Cashew
    Soup with
    Pomegranate Seeds,
    53
  Celery Root, Chestnut,
    and Gorgonzola
    Soup, 132
  Circassian Chicken
    Soup, 186
  Dukkah, 49
  Radish Greens Soup
    with Toasted
    Hazelnuts, 139
  Spiced Rutabaga-Apple
    Soup, 88
  West African Peanut
    Soup with Chicken,
    137
  Wild Mushroom Soup,
    87

O
Okra
  Louisiana Sausage and
    Chicken Gumbo, 213

Onion(s)
  Belgian Beef, Beer, and
    Vegetable Soup, 202
  chopping, 24
  -Leek and Shallot
    Bisque, Creamy, 90
  slicing, 23–24
  Strings, Frizzled, 69
Oranges
  Chilled Strawberry-
    Ginger Soup, 28
  Provençal Tomato-
    Fennel Soup with
    Saffron, 74
Orzo and Chicken-
  Vegetable Soup, 171
Oyster Soup, Creamy,
  with Lemon-Parsley
  Pesto, 150

P
Pancetta
  Gascon Duck Confit
    and Vegetable Soup,
    190
  White Bean, Vegetable,
    and Sun-Dried
    Tomato Soup, 118
Parmesan
  Bruce's Homemade
    Basil Pesto, 44
  Lemon-Parsley Pesto,
    151
  Mom's Minestrone, 93
  Nonna's Rice and
    Potato Soup, 84
  Pistou, 70
  -Pumpernickel
    Croutons, 114
Parsley
  -Lemon Pesto, 151
  Pistou, 70
Parsnip(s)
  cutting, 24
  Moroccan Tomato-
    Chickpea Soup, 128
  Prosciutto, and Potato
    Soup, 200

"Silk Purse" Roasted Leftover Root Vegetable Soup, 95
Vegetarian Split Green Pea Soup, 112
Peach Soup with Sugar-Glazed Blackberries, 32
Peanut butter
  South American Pork, Peppers, and Black Bean Soup, 206
  West African Peanut Soup with Chicken, 137
Peanut Soup, West African, with Chicken, 137
Pea(s)
  Belgian Beef, Beer, and Vegetable Soup, 202
  Chicken-Vegetable and Orzo Soup, 171
  Chinese Noodle Soup with Shrimp, 161
  Green, Soup, Minted Spiced, with Crunchy Chickpeas, 57
  Green Vegetable Soup with Pistou, 70
Pecorino-Romano cheese
  Bruce's Homemade Basil Pesto, 44
Pepper(s). See also Chile(s)
  Gazpacho, 60
  and Mole, Butternut Squash Soup with, 64
  Plantains, and Coconut, Jamaican Jerk Chicken Soup with, 176
  Pork, and Black Bean Soup, South American, 206
  Red, –Roasted Tomato Soup, Spicy, with Salted Basil Cream, 77

slicing or dicing, 24
Spanish Red Lentil and Chorizo Soup, 108
Pernod
  Provençal Mussel Soup, 147
  Provençal Tomato-Fennel Soup with Saffron, 74
Pesto
  Basil, Bruce's Homemade, 44
  Chilled Summer Tomato Soup with, 43
  Lemon-Parsley, 151
Pineapple
  Jamaican Jerk Chicken Soup with Coconut, Plantains, and Peppers, 176
  peeling and cutting, 35
  Soup with Blueberries and Toasted Coconut, 35
Pine nuts
  Bruce's Homemade Basil Pesto, 44
  Pistou, 70
  Turkish Eggplant Soup, 96
Pistachios
  Dukkah, 49
  Pistou, 70
Pistou, 70
Plantains
  about, 177
  Coconut, and Peppers, Jamaican Jerk Chicken Soup with, 176
Pomegranate
  -Blueberry Beet Borscht, 31
  Seeds, Cauliflower-Cashew Soup with, 53
Pork. See also Bacon; Ham; Sausage(s)

Mexican Meatball Soup in Red Chile–Tomato Broth, 216–17
Peppers, and Black Bean Soup, South American, 206
Southwestern Chili Soup, 199
Posole, Shrimp, 154
Potato(es)
  Clam, and Kale Soup with Bacon, 144
  Finnish Jerusalem Artichoke Soup with Marinated Tofu, 103
  Kale, Tofu, and Sun-Dried Tomato Soup, 73
  Leek, and Tomato Soup, Chunky, 76
  Minted Spiced Green Pea Soup with Crunchy Chickpeas, 57
  Parsnip, and Prosciutto Soup, 200
  Radish Greens Soup with Toasted Hazelnuts, 139
  and Rice Soup, Nonna's, 84
  Seafood Chowder, 158
Poultry soups
  Chicken Soup for the Soul, 168
  Chicken-Vegetable and Orzo Soup, 171
  Circassian Chicken Soup, 186
  Far Better Than Canned Chicken Noodle Soup, 166
  Gascon Duck Confit and Vegetable Soup, 190
  Greek Lemon Chicken and Rice Soup, 165
  Jamaican Jerk Chicken

Soup with Coconut, Plantains, and Peppers, 176
Japanese Chicken and Noodle Soup, 172
Leftover Turkey and Tomatillo Soup, 188
Malaysian Chicken Laksa, 175
Mexican Chicken Tortilla Soup, 179
Scottish Cock-a-Leekie Soup, 180
Thai Chicken and Coconut Milk Soup, 185
Prosciutto, Parsnip, and Potato Soup, 200
Provençal Mussel Soup, 147
Provençal Tomato-Fennel Soup with Saffron, 74
Pumpkin
Black Bean, and Tomato Soup, 117
-Coconut Soup, Curried, 98
Seeds, Chile-Spiced, 115
Puréed Avocado Soup with Guacamole Toppings, 47

Q
Queso fresco
about, 217
Mexican Chicken Tortilla Soup, 179
Mexican Meatball Soup in Red Chile–Tomato Broth, 216–17
Quick Vegetable Soup, 25

R
Radish Greens Soup with Toasted Hazelnuts, 139
Rainy Day Tomato Bisque with Mini Cheese

Triangles, 79
Ras al Hanout, about, 95
Rice
flour, about, 67
and Lemon Chicken Soup, Greek, 165
and Potato Soup, Nonna's, 84
Roasted Beet Soup with Dukkah, Yogurt, and Black Currant, 48
Rosemary and Asiago Crostini, 119
Rum
Jamaican Jerk Chicken Soup with Coconut, Plantains, and Peppers, 176
Pineapple Soup with Blueberries and Toasted Coconut, 35
Thai Mango-Shrimp Soup, 157
Rutabaga
about, 88
-Apple Soup, Spiced, 88
slicing and cutting, 88

S
Saffron
Provençal Mussel Soup, 147
Provençal Tomato-Fennel Soup with, 74
Salad bar ingredients, 19–20
Salmon and Corn Chowder, 153
Sausage, Lamb, White Bean, and Garlic Soup, 195
Sausage(s)
and Chicken Gumbo, Louisiana, 213
Gascon Duck Confit and Vegetable Soup, 190

Italian, Yam, and Spinach Soup, 196
Spanish Chorizo-Garlic Soup, 209
Spanish Red Lentil and Chorizo Soup, 108
Spanish vs. Mexican chorizo, 108
and Yellow Split Pea Soup, 210
Scallion(s)
Chinese Noodle Soup with Shrimp, 161
and Cucumber Soup, Curried, 51
Japanese Chicken and Noodle Soup, 172
Scallop(s)
and Kale Soup, 142
Sea, and Lobster Chowder, Spanish, 143
Seafood Chowder, 158
Scottish Cock-a-Leekie Soup, 180
Seafood soups
Chinese Noodle Soup with Shrimp, 161
Clam, Potato, and Kale Soup with Bacon, 144
Creamy Oyster Soup with Lemon-Parsley Pesto, 150
Provençal Mussel Soup, 147
Salmon and Corn Chowder, 153
Scallop and Kale Soup, 142
Seafood Chowder, 158
Shrimp Posole, 154
Spanish Lobster and Sea Scallop Chowder, 143
Thai Coconut-Mussel Soup, 148
Thai Mango-Shrimp Soup, 157

Sesame seeds
  Dukkah, 49
Shallot and Onion-Leek
  Bisque, Creamy, 90
Shellfish
  Chinese Noodle Soup
    with Shrimp, 161
  Clam, Potato, and Kale
    Soup with Bacon,
    144
  Creamy Oyster Soup
    with Lemon-Parsley
    Pesto, 150
  Provençal Mussel Soup,
    147
  Scallop and Kale Soup,
    142
  Seafood Chowder, 158
  Shrimp Posole, 154
  Spanish Lobster
    and Sea Scallop
    Chowder, 143
  Thai Carrot-Ginger
    Soup, 100
  Thai Coconut-Mussel
    Soup, 148
  Thai Mango-Shrimp
    Soup, 157
  Watermelon Gazpacho
    Soup, 39
Sherry
  Black Bean, Pumpkin,
    and Tomato Soup,
    117
  Creamy Onion-Leek
    and Shallot Bisque,
    90
Shrimp
  Chinese Noodle Soup
    with, 161
  -Mango Soup, Thai,
    157
  Posole, 154
  Seafood Chowder, 158
  Thai Carrot-Ginger
    Soup, 100
"Silk Purse" Roasted
  Leftover Root

Vegetable Soup, 95
Soba Noodles, Tofu,
  Shiitakes, and Bok
  Choy, Miso Soup with,
  81
Soups
  adding leftovers to, 24
  buying ingredients for,
    19–20
  cutting and chopping
    vegetables for,
    23–24
  equipment for, 16
  measuring ingredients
    for, 23
  stocks and broths for,
    20
  thickening, with masa
    harina, 198
  thickening, with rice
    flour, 67
  using every part of the
    vegetable, 24
South American Pork,
  Peppers, and Black
  Bean Soup, 206
Southwestern Chili Soup,
  199
Spanish Chorizo-Garlic
  Soup, 209
Spanish Lobster and Sea
  Scallop Chowder, 143
Spanish Red Lentil and
  Chorizo Soup, 108
Spiced Rutabaga-Apple
  Soup, 88
Spicy Roasted Tomato–
  Red Pepper Soup with
  Salted Basil Cream, 77
Spinach
  Italian Sausage, and
    Yam Soup, 196
  and Turkey-Barley
    Soup, 124
Split Green Pea Soup,
  Vegetarian, 112
Split Pea, Yellow, and
  Sausage Soup, 210

Squash
  Black Bean, Pumpkin,
    and Tomato Soup,
    117
  Butternut, Balsamic-
    Glazed, and Goat
    Cheese, Lentil Soup
    with, 107
  Butternut, Soup with
    Mole and Peppers,
    64
  Curried Pumpkin-
    Coconut Soup, 98
  Green Vegetable Soup
    with Pistou, 70
  Mom's Minestrone, 93
Stocks, 20
Strawberry-Ginger Soup,
  Chilled, 28

T
Thai Carrot-Ginger Soup,
  100
Thai Chicken and
  Coconut Milk Soup, 185
Thai Coconut-Mussel
  Soup, 148
Thai Mango-Shrimp
  Soup, 157
Tofu
  Japanese Chicken and
    Noodle Soup, 172
  Kale, Potato, and
    Sun-Dried Tomato
    Soup, 73
  Marinated, Finnish
    Jerusalem Artichoke
    Soup with, 103
  Shiitakes, Bok Choy,
    and Soba Noodles,
    Miso Soup with, 81
Tomatillo(s)
  and Leftover Turkey
    Soup, 188
  Mexican Meatball Soup
    in Red Chile–Tomato
    Broth, 216–17
  Shrimp Posole, 154

Tomato(es)
  Bisque, Rainy Day,
    with Mini Cheese
    Triangles, 79
  Black Bean, and
    Pumpkin Soup, 117
  -Chickpea Soup,
    Moroccan, 128
  Diced, Cucumber-
    Watercress Soup
    with, 61
  -Fennel Soup,
    Provençal, with
    Saffron, 74
  Fire-Roasted, Bisque,
    Chilled, 40
  Gazpacho, 60
  Hearty Turkey-
    Vegetable-Bean
    Soup, 127
  Leek, and Potato Soup,
    Chunky, 76
  Louisiana Sausage and
    Chicken Gumbo, 213
  Mexican Chicken
    Tortilla Soup, 179
  Mom's Minestrone, 93
  Provençal Mussel Soup,
    147
  Puréed Avocado Soup
    with Guacamole
    Toppings, 47
  –Red Chile Broth,
    Mexican Meatball
    Soup in, 216–17
  Roasted, –Red Pepper
    Soup, Spicy, with
    Salted Basil Cream,
    77
  Soup, Chilled Summer,
    with Pesto, 43
  Southwestern Chili
    Soup, 199
  Sun-Dried, Kale, Potato,
    and Tofu Soup, 73
  Sun-Dried, White Bean,
    and Vegetable Soup,
    118

Two, –Double Chickpea
    Soup, 121
Tortilla(s)
  Chicken Soup, Mexican,
    179
  Puréed Avocado Soup
    with Guacamole
    Toppings, 47
  Strips, Crispy, 189
Turkey
  -Barley and Spinach
    Soup, 124
  Leftover, and Tomatillo
    Soup, 188
  -Vegetable-Bean Soup,
    Hearty, 127
Turkish Eggplant Soup,
  96

V
Vegetable(s). See also
  specific vegetables
  buying at salad bars,
    19–20
  cutting and chopping,
    23–24
  measuring, note about,
    23
  using every part of, 24
Vegetable soups
  Butternut Squash
    Soup with Mole and
    Peppers, 64
  Carrot-Ginger Soup
    with Chèvre, 67
  Chunky Leek, Potato,
    and Tomato Soup,
    76
  Creamy Onion-Leek
    and Shallot Bisque,
    90
  Curried Pumpkin-
    Coconut Soup, 98
  Finnish Jerusalem
    Artichoke Soup with
    Marinated Tofu, 103
  Green Bean–Mushroom
    Soup with Frizzled

  Onion Strings, 68
  Green Vegetable Soup
    with Pistou, 70
  Kale, Potato, Tofu, and
    Sun-Dried Tomato
    Soup, 73
  Miso Soup with Tofu,
    Shiitakes, Bok Choy,
    and Soba Noodles,
    81
  Mom's Minestrone, 93
  Nonna's Rice and
    Potato Soup, 84
  Provençal Tomato-
    Fennel Soup with
    Saffron, 74
  Quick Vegetable Soup,
    25
  Rainy Day Tomato
    Bisque with Mini
    Cheese Triangles, 79
  "Silk Purse" Roasted
    Leftover Root
    Vegetable Soup, 95
  Spiced Rutabaga-Apple
    Soup, 88
  Spicy Roasted Tomato–
    Red Pepper Soup
    with Salted Basil
    Cream, 77
  Thai Carrot-Ginger
    Soup, 100
  Turkish Eggplant Soup,
    96
  Wild Mushroom Soup,
    87
Vegetarian Split Green
  Pea Soup, 112

W
Walnuts
  Circassian Chicken
    Soup, 186
  Spiced Rutabaga-Apple
    Soup, 88
Watercress-Cucumber
  Soup with Diced
  Tomatoes, 61

Watermelon
    Andalusian Garlic-
        Almond Soup, 54
    Gazpacho Soup, 39
West African Peanut
    Soup with Chicken, 137
Wild Mushroom Soup, 87

Y

Yam, Italian Sausage, and
    Spinach Soup, 196

Yellow Split Pea and
    Sausage Soup, 210
Yogurt
    Chilled Strawberry-
        Ginger Soup, 28
    Cucumber-Watercress
        Soup with Diced
        Tomatoes, 61
    Dukkah, and Black
        Currant, Roasted
        Beet Soup with, 48

-Harissa Drizzle, 129
Peach Soup with Sugar-
    Glazed Blackberries,
    32

Z

Zucchini
    Green Vegetable Soup
        with Pistou, 70
    Mom's Minestrone, 93